Ploughshares and

Matt,

Ploughshares and First Fruits

A Year of Festivals for the Rural Church

Chris Thorpe

CANTERBURY
PRESS
Norwich

First published in 2020 by the Canterbury Press Norwich
Editorial office
3rd Floor, Invicta House
108–114 Golden Lane
London EC1Y 0TG, UK
www.canterburypress.co.uk

Canterbury Press is an imprint of Hymns Ancient & Modern Ltd (a registered charity)

Hymns Ancient & Modern® is a registered trademark of
Hymns Ancient & Modern Ltd
13A Hellesdon Park Road, Norwich,
Norfolk NR6 5DR, UK

The author and publisher acknowledge with thanks permission to use copyright
poetry: Malcolm Guite, 'Daily Bread', in *Parable and Paradox*, Canterbury Press, 2016
Malcolm Guite, 'Mothering Sunday', in *Sounding the Seasons*, Canterbury Press, 2012.

Scripture quotations are from New Revised Standard Version Bible: Anglicized
Edition, copyright © 1989, 1995 National Council of the Churches of Christ in the
United States of America.
Used by permission. All rights reserved worldwide.

British Library Cataloguing in Publication data

A catalogue record for this book is available
from the British Library

978 1 78622 290 9

Typeset by Regent Typesetting
Printed and bound in Great Britain by
CPI Group (UK) Ltd

Contents

Dedicated to
Sarah, Sophie and Jake
and with thanks to Rachel.

Introduction

Ploughshares and First Fruits explores traditional agricultural feasts, new countryside festivals, saints' days and themes to bring rural communities together in worship.

How do we get rural churches to grow? How do we connect with our communities again when churches can sometimes seem to have been left behind? For many it will only be at Christmas or the Harvest Festival when we see the pews filling up. Sunday by Sunday, it may be only a handful who come to worship, very often an increasingly aged congregation. Rural churches are today often part of multi-parish groupings with clergy spread very thin, trying to cover the ground, and worship frequently needs to be locally planned and led by people other than the clergy. Of course, these issues are not limited to rural churches: many in urban and suburban communities will see the same picture.

What are we offering people when they come to church? Sometimes the words and music, the themes and concerns seem disconnected from the reality of people's lives. Much of our worship assumes a level of knowledge of the Christian faith that people no longer have. Many today also want to be involved, to participate, not simply to listen in a passive way to what is presented. Some of our worship can be very wordy, very 'head-level', and can fail to connect with the heart, with the lived experience of people's lives.

Ploughshares and First Fruits is a mission-led response to some of these questions and realities, offering stepping stones, opening connections between the heart of our own lives and the heart of faith. It contains resources for hard-pressed church leaders, whether clergy or not, to enable churches to reconnect with the local community. It seeks to draw the occasional visitor, who might attend church at Christmas, Easter, Harvest and Remembrance, to attend on a more regular basis, perhaps at a monthly 'festival'. It provides suggestions for involving people in preparations before the service, as well as participating in music, readings, prayers and reflections in the service itself.

We have been using this approach for the past ten years in three parishes in rural Shropshire and it has been fruitful. The aim is to offer worship that is well prepared, that has involved a wide number of people in its creation and that connects with real lives and concerns. The aim is also to go deeper, to enable people to make real connections with the good news of God's love so that our lives are changed by the experience. Jesus used parables to connect with people and to challenge them. Often, he used instances from rural life, like the sowing of seed, the harvesting of crops or the managing of animals, to illustrate a deeper message about our walk with God. But these rural illustrations are not simply a way of celebrating country life! When Jesus tells a parable it provides a bridge, a way in, to a deeper conversation with our communities and with God. It offers a question to think about, a challenge to take away, an opportunity for transformation.

This book contains outlines of 24 festival services, providing two years' worth of material if festival services are offered once a month. It is for each church to decide what it feels it can offer wholeheartedly, so it may be appropriate to hold these festival services less often, spread over a longer period. Each service follows a similar pattern of resources.

Preparation and invitation

Start by drawing together a group to plan and prepare for the service. Each festival begins with a suggestion of how to engage people beforehand, to enable them to participate in some way. It encourages proper advertising and promotion of the event, using the power of invitation to encourage people to come. From good old-fashioned word of mouth to the latest social media, we need to find ways of reaching out beyond the usual people who attend church. There may be local organizations that will share our interests and values and be pleased to take part, or we may be able to involve individuals or companies who have a stake in the issues we focus on. Even if you create the best service in the world, its impact will be limited unless people come to share it. So preparation and publicity, engagement and invitation, are all essential.

In a rural area, it is likely that there will be a folk memory of some of the traditional agricultural festivals of the year. Plough Sunday, Rogation, Lammas and Harvest Festival are all important moments in the farming year. To reawaken the traditional connections between farming and worship, you may choose to write to all the farmers and farmworkers in your area, specifically inviting them to the services. The National Farmers' Union may be willing to help to compile this list, or a friendly local farmer may assist. A letter can give an opportunity to say how much the farming community is valued, and to stress the important role it plays in the community. Other interest groups may also share some of our values and concerns, so it is worth thinking about how you can engage them in these festivals: consider any local National Trust properties or land, nature conservancy and wildlife groups, groups that value the countryside and the natural environment, walking and rambling groups.

Welcome and hospitality

Even for those who already come to church occasionally, it can be daunting to come to a church service. So give some thought to the welcome! For some of our festival services, we have chosen to share a simple breakfast ahead of the service. Bacon sandwiches or pancakes work well. People can make connections over breakfast, in a relaxed social environment, sharing conversations and naturally catching up with local news. New folks can be welcomed over a cuppa. On a practical note, the time around breakfast can give anyone who is taking part in the worship time to check out their role and place in the service.

It can help to have some background music playing as people arrive, to overcome the silence or formality of church that is sometimes off-putting. Gathering music is suggested for each service. In one church locally, a community choir has formed to support these festival services: they are often rehearsing as people arrive, which can make it very easy to share or teach a new song or hymn.

Sacred space

Church buildings can be places of great beauty and atmosphere: this can help people to find the mental space to connect with their deeper selves and with God. There are suggestions as to the layout and visual focus for each service. Sometimes a simple visual image can convey so much and help people to make new connections. The transition into worship is important to manage – it may be helpful for someone leading worship to introduce a time of silence to help people to prepare. Just as God called Moses to remove his shoes as he approached the burning bush, so it is important that we enable people to approach worship with a sense of expectation, a sense of awe and of wonder. Silence is such a rare thing in many people's lives today: we can easily fill every spare moment with noise. In these services, there will be time for silence and reflection: sometimes, silence can speak to us more deeply than the most eloquent of words!

Hymns and music

There are suggestions for music to be played at various points in the festival services, to give space or to allow time for movement. Choose from a range of hymns, songs and chants to suit your local church or congregation, whether traditional or contemporary, for young or old. These suggestions are not exhaustive, so feel free to use other music that might be better for your local situation. Hymns, chants and songs should be chosen to be sing-able! If there are local musicians available, why not invite them to play in the service or to accompany the singing? It is important that there is enough music that is familiar to people to make them feel they can join in. Any unfamiliar items should be taught at the beginning of the service.

Reflection and conversation

Each festival service includes Bible readings and short reflections to go with them. Sometimes a reading from another discipline has been included to give an insight into the theme. Readings from science or from history, especially local history, can be helpful to show how the good news of God's love is not separate from the real lives we live and the real places to which we belong. Sometimes poems convey a deeper truth than prose can ever manage. There may even be a local poet who could write something for the occasion.

Long sermons and complicated theology or doctrine can alienate people, and easily leave the congregation as passive recipients. On the other hand, there is a danger of offering religious entertainment rather than engagement. A short reflection followed by a brief conversation around a key question can be both participative and informative and may possibly lead to real change in a person's attitude or action. The reflections are not intended to be printed: they are there to help whoever is leading that section of the service.

It can help to have some people unobtrusively move and sit near to a new person, to make conversations as easy as possible.

Symbolic action

For each festival service there is a time of action. In some services this is a symbolic action that helps to reinforce the theme of the service, inviting people to bring their own personal concerns to God; in others it may be a way of embodying our response to God through commitment to change. At its best, worship engages us as whole people: body, mind, heart and spirit. So as well as involving our minds in thought and reflection, and allowing time to make connections with our hearts, we seek to embody our worship to engage our physical senses. It can help us to have something tangible to take away, a visible reminder of the good news of God's love for each person in their own particular situation. This can help anchor the theme, reflection and conversation in our memories, and be a continuing reminder at home of any commitment to change that we may have made.

Prayers and responses

For each service a framework of possible prayers and responses is provided. However, it is important that people feel free to create their own words if they wish, and to be confident in using them: the most powerful prayers arise out of the context of those praying.

The services include prayers and responses that seek to avoid formal religious or doctrinal language. They are intended to arise from human experience and to use language that is familiar, yet also to connect with the biblical text. Those leading prayers and responses are encouraged to take the pace slowly, speaking with meaning and feeling. The prayers should be spacious and unhurried, giving time for people to hear and understand, making their own connections with the words.

Eucharist or not?

In some churches, it will be important to face the question of whether the service should include the Eucharist. If we want new people to try coming to church, we need to put ourselves in their shoes: a Eucharist can make the service quite long and can exclude those who are new to faith or just dipping their toe in the water. We choose to make these festival services non-eucharistic and all-age, seeing them as a means of outreach in the wider community. However, if it is decided to include the Eucharist, it is possible to use the festival service format as the Ministry of the Word and to add the Peace and a Eucharistic Prayer to complete the service.

JANUARY

Holy White Birds

Plough Sunday – Blessing the plough and the ploughman

Preparation and Invitation

You may like to contact local farmers and farmworkers to invite them personally to this service. Farmers could be asked to take part, reading or being interviewed. You could locate a traditional plough to have in church and/or a modern plough for outside the church.

Gathering Music – *suggestion*

Warhorse – Ploughing theme, John Williams

Welcome and Introduction

We come to give thanks for the fertility of our land, to pray for a good harvest and to bless the plough and the ploughmen and women of our community. So much has changed in farming, from horse-drawn single furrow-ploughing, to eight-share machines of great power, and now to minimum tillage where we plough the land less often to retain the soil structure. Plough Sunday is also a time to think of our own lives, of what needs to be cut through, of what needs to be overturned, of what we may need to do to create a fruitful environment for our living and our loving, in our own lives, homes and communities.

Hymn/Song – *suggestions*

For the beauty of the earth, Folliott Sandford Pierpoint

O give thanks to the Lord, Graham Kendrick

Creation sings the Father's song, Keith Getty, Kristyn Getty, Stuart Townend

Opening Responses

Bless the Lord, O my soul.
O Lord my God, you are very great.
You cause the grass to grow for the cattle,
and plants for people to use,
to bring forth food from the earth,
and wine to gladden the human heart,
oil to make the face shine,
and bread to strengthen the human heart.
Psalm 104.1, 14, 15

Reading – *'Daily Bread', Malcolm Guite*

Give us this day our daily bread we pray,
As though it came straight from the hand of God,
As though we held an empty plate each day,
And found it filled, by miracle, with food,
Although we know the ones who plough and sow,
Who pick and plant and package whilst we sleep
With slow backbreaking labour, row by row,
And send away to others all they reap,

We know that these unseen who meet our needs
Are all themselves the fingers of your hand,
As are the grain, the rain, the air, the land,
And, slighting these, we slight the hand that feeds.
What if we glimpsed you daily in their toil
And found and thanked and served you through them all?

Reflection

Malcolm Guite reminds us of all the work that goes on unseen to bring food to our plates. He makes the connection that God is working through the hands of the farmer, the pickers, the packager, to 'give us this day our daily bread'. He points to the presence of God in 'the grain, the rain, the air, the land'.

In his poem 'The Everlasting Mercy', John Masefield captures the essence of the horse-drawn plough, in its task of 'turning a stubborn clay to fruit', breaking open the land to make it fertile, cutting through the 'rest-harrow and bitter roots', to give space for the harvest to grow.

It is the same task in our own hearts and lives: we need to be opened up to God; the weeds need cutting through, to allow us to grow and change. The poem continues with the words of our next hymn, 'O Christ who holds the open gate': these words recognize Christ not just in church but in the fields, in the plough, in the soil, in the ploughing, in everything. For Masefield there is no separation of sacred and secular, church and world, work and prayer: all is one!

Hymn – *suggestion*

O Christ who holds the open gate, John Masefield (an easy tune is Gonfalon Royal)

Interview with a Farmer

How has ploughing changed in your lifetime?

Blessing of the Soil and Plough

Farmer: Anyone who tills the land will have plenty of bread,
All: **but one who follows worthless pursuits will have plenty of poverty.**
Proverbs 28.19

Farmer: See now, I am for you; I will turn to you,
All: **and you shall be tilled and sown.**
Ezekiel 36.9

Farmer: They shall beat their swords into ploughshares,
and their spears into pruning-hooks;

All: they shall all sit under their own vines and under their own
           fig trees,
           and no one shall make them afraid;
           for the mouth of the Lord of hosts has spoken.
           Micah 4.3–4

The service leader takes a handful of soil and says:

May this soil represent all the land, all the fields, all the soil,
   of this community.
May God bless the soil, make it fruitful, bringing a sustainable harvest.
May God bless those who till the soil, giving them wisdom to care for
   its health.
May we all honour the land by our stewardship of creation.
God bless the soil.
God bless the soil.

The service leader lays a hand on the plough and says:

May this plough represent all the equipment and machinery used in
   farming this land.
May God bless the plough, as it cuts through the compacted earth,
breaking through roots and weeds, feeding and conditioning the soil.
Bless us in our choice of what to plough and what to leave unploughed.
May we all honour the land by our stewardship of creation.
God speed the plough.
God speed the plough!

Hymn/Song – *suggestions*

> God, whose farm is all creation, John Arlott

> Lord, bring the day to pass, Ian Masson Fraser

> Touch the earth lightly, Shirley Erena Murray

Bible Reading – *Luke 9.57–62*

> As they were going along the road, someone said to him, 'I will follow
> you wherever you go.' And Jesus said to him, 'Foxes have holes, and
> birds of the air have nests; but the Son of Man has nowhere to lay
> his head.' To another he said, 'Follow me.' But he said, 'Lord, first
> let me go and bury my father.' But Jesus said to him, 'Let the dead

bury their own dead; but as for you, go and proclaim the kingdom of God.' Another said, 'I will follow you, Lord; but let me first say farewell to those at my home.' Jesus said to him, 'No one who puts a hand to the plough and looks back is fit for the kingdom of God.'

Living Word of God,
live in us today.

Reflection

Jesus talked about God and the life of faith using examples taken from everyday life and work that would have been very familiar to his hearers. We sometimes make rash promises or overambitious commitments and find we can't live up to them. 'I will follow you wherever you go.' Sometimes we can hear the call of God 'follow me', but we make excuses and don't follow through. The image of trying to plough looking backwards is a comic one! To plough a straight furrow, to live a fruitful life, we need to keep our eyes fixed on an unchanging 'mark'. Jesus calls us to follow him, to take up the plough, to cut through all the matted roots and weeds in our lives, to break open our hardened hearts, to allow his new life to grow in us.

Silence *(two minutes)*

In the silence we hold these questions:

Do I tend to look backwards or forwards in my life?
What are the roots and weeds that I need to cut through?
What is the harvest I am hoping for?
What can I do now to prepare the soil?

Music for Reflection – *suggestion*

Warhorse – Ploughing theme, John Williams

Action

Take two sticky notes, one orange and one green.
On the orange note, write one thing that needs to be cut through or
    overturned for you to be able to be fruitful in your life.

On the green note, write your hope as you prepare the soil for the coming harvest.

As the music begins, come up and stick them on to the plough.

Music – *suggestion*

Warhorse – Ploughing theme, John Williams

Hymn/Song/Chant – *suggestions*

The kingdom of God is justice and peace, Taizé Community

O Lord, listen to my prayer, Margaret Rizza

Be still and know that I am God, Unknown, based on Psalm 46

Prayers of Recognition

We bring to God all that needs cutting through in our lives,
all that limits our fruitfulness,
the worry, fear, resentment and guilt,
the memories and hurts that have distorted us.
(Silence)

Through rest-harrow and bitter roots,
plough in my heart.

We bring to God all that needs turning over in our lives,
all that prevents us from growing and changing,
the habits and dependencies, the addictions and avoidances,
all that prevents us from being our true selves.
(Silence)

Through rest-harrow and bitter roots,
plough in my heart.

We bring to God all that needs breaking open in our lives,
all that has become hardened in us,
the prejudices we harbour, the attitudes we never question,
all that distances us from one another and from God.
(Silence)

Through rest-harrow and bitter roots,
plough in my heart.

Prayers of Intercession

For all who farm the land, all who plough the soil,
all who feed our nation,
we pray that their work may be fruitful
and their stewardship of the land may be sustainable.
(Silence)

Fix our eyes on your mark of love,
guide us to make the furrow straight.

For landowners and politicians, all who decide policy,
all who make decisions about farming practices,
we pray that they may sustain diversity in the natural world
and respect the balance of nature.
(Silence)

Fix our eyes on your mark of love,
guide us to make the furrow straight.

For supermarkets and commodity traders, all who influence
    the market,
all who set standards and maximize their profits,
we pray that they may recognize the work of the farming community
and give proper value to the harvest.
(Silence)

Fix our eyes on your mark of love,
guide us to make the furrow straight.

For ourselves as consumers, who have the power to choose,
we pray that we might recognize the true cost of low prices,
and learn to be less wasteful of our food,
to use our power to influence the market, for the common good.
(Silence)

Fix our eyes on your mark of love,
guide us to make the furrow straight.

We pray for all farmers struggling with ill health, stress and isolation,
and for all who work to support the farming community,
the Farming Community Networks, Rural Action and the National
    Farmers' Union.
(Silence)

Fix our eyes on your mark of love,
guide us to make the furrow straight.

Hymn – *suggestions*

As the days begin to lengthen, Stephen Southgate

Sing out, earth and skies, Marty Haugen

Blessing

O Christ who holds the open gate,
open the gate of our hearts to your love.
O Christ who drives the furrow straight,
guide our living and our loving by your mark of love.
O Christ the plough,
cut through all that limits us, overturn our wilfulness.
O Christ the laughter of holy white birds flying after,
awaken us to the laughter of all creation, in harmony with you.
May the blessing of almighty God,
the Father, the Son and the Holy Spirit,
be always with us. **Amen.**

Mosaic of Grace

Week of Prayer for Christian Unity –
Seeing the whole picture

Preparation and Invitation

The Week of Prayer for Christian Unity takes place each year from 18 to 25 January. There is usually a booklet with suggested themes and prayers produced by Churches Together in Britain and Ireland. This service is intended to complement the official material and to offer a slightly different way into this important ecumenical event. You might like to write to all the different Christian denominations in your area, inviting them to help prepare for the service and to publicize it to their members.

Each person attending will be invited to bring some broken fragments of pottery or china, an old teapot lid, an odd saucer, some buttons and so forth. These will be combined to create a mosaic during the service. If you have a local art teacher or art group, you could ask them to take a lead in planning and helping in the service.

You will need glue and filler or grouting material suitable for fixing tiles, and a wooden base with a raised lip to contain the picture. You may like to plan out the mosaic by drawing a design on the board beforehand. It could be a word such as TOGETHER or a phrase, MAY THEY BE ONE. It could be a picture of a fish, a cross or a Celtic pattern.

Gathering Music – *suggestion*

Goodness of God, Jenn Johnson

Welcome and Introduction

We come together to celebrate the many Christian denominations that make up the worldwide body of Christ. We are different in so many ways! Our traditions and histories have shaped us, given us each a distinctive flavour. St Paul encouraged us to value those differences, knowing that together, though we are many, we are one body, in Christ. On our own we can see only part of the picture, but together we can begin to glimpse the big picture of God's love for the whole world. So we join our many voices to sing God's praise.

Hymn – *suggestions*

Family of Faith, Steven Ottományi

Great God your love has called us here, Brian Wren

Opening Responses

For as in one body we have many members,
and not all the members have the same function,
so we, who are many, are one body in Christ,
and individually we are members one of another.
We have gifts that differ according to the grace given to us:
prophecy, in proportion to faith;
ministry, in ministering;
the teacher, in teaching;
the exhorter, in exhortation;
the giver, in generosity;
the leader, in diligence;
the compassionate, in cheerfulness.
Thanks be to God! Amen. Amen.
Romans 12.4–8

Reading

Mosaic art was popular in Roman times: images made up of many small pieces of tile, in different shapes and colours, but together making a larger picture. A Christian family would often  have a mosaic picture of a fish set into the floor, symbolizing the secret Christian sign *ichthus*, in Greek signifying 'Jesus Christ, Son of God, Saviour'. To make the whole picture every tile is needed, each colour, each shape, each size – all are needed to make up the whole. So in this week of prayer for Christian unity, each of our denominations are needed, with all our different styles and insights, all our traditions and distinctive gifts. The Bible talks of our gift as a *charism* (1 John 2.20): our particular gift and calling from the Holy Spirit. Unity is never about uniformity; it is always about learning to value our differences! You can hear some of this in Gerard Manley Hopkins's poem 'Pied Beauty'.

Reading – *'Pied Beauty', Gerard Manley Hopkins*

Glory be to God for dappled things –
For skies of couple-colour as a brinded cow;
For rose-moles all in stipple upon trout that swim;
Fresh-firecoal chestnut-falls; finches' wings;
Landscape plotted and pieced – fold, fallow, and plough;
And all trades, their gear and tackle and trim.

All things counter, original, spare, strange;
Whatever is fickle, freckled (who knows how?)
With swift, slow; sweet, sour; adazzle, dim;
He fathers-forth whose beauty is past change:
Praise him.

Litany of Thanksgiving

We give thanks for the breadth and diversity of God's charism in our many churches.
For the Baptist Church, honouring an adult decision to follow Jesus:
I thank my God every time I remember you.
For the Salvation Army, serving the poor, showing love in practical ways:
I thank my God every time I remember you.
For the Methodist Church, reaching out with scriptural holiness, and gift of singing:
I thank my God every time I remember you.
For the Roman Catholic Church, holding liturgy and sacrament for all nations:
I thank my God every time I remember you.
For the Society of Friends, the Quakers, who remind us of silence and justice:
I thank my God every time I remember you.

For the Orthodox Church, holding truth through mystery and tradition:
I thank my God every time I remember you.
For the United Reformed Church, seeking unity, always questioning,
ready to challenge:
I thank my God every time I remember you.
For Evangelical and Free Churches, with a passion to share the good
news with all:
I thank my God every time I remember you.
For Pentecostal and Charismatic Churches, alive to the Spirit, in
freedom of worship:
I thank my God every time I remember you.
For the Anglican Church, seeking the middle way, embracing all
people, our national church:
I thank my God every time I remember you.
(You may like to add other churches that are appropriate in your area.)

I thank my God every time I remember you, constantly praying with
joy in every one of my prayers for all of you, because of your sharing
in the gospel from the first day until now.
Philippians 1.3–5

Prayers of Regret

Where we have looked down on one another,
where we have not recognized God's gift in one another,
where we have thought our way was the only way:
Lord, have mercy.
Christ, have mercy.
Lord, have mercy.

Give us grace to grow into the full image of your love,
to show the power of forgiveness and reconciliation,
in a broken and divided world.
May we be one,
as you are one, O God.
Amen.

Hymn – *suggestions*

There's a wideness in God's mercy, Frederick William Faber

Lord, we come to ask your healing, Jean Holloway

Bible Reading – *John 17.20–24 – Jesus' own prayer to the Father*

I ask not only on behalf of these, but also on behalf of those who will believe in me through their word, that they may all be one. As you, Father, are in me and I am in you, may they also be in us, so that the world may believe that you have sent me. The glory that you have given me I have given them, so that they may be one, as we are one, I in them and you in me, that they may become completely one, so that the world may know that you have sent me and have loved them even as you have loved me. Father, I desire that those also, whom you have given me, may be with me where I am, to see my glory, which you have given me because you loved me before the foundation of the world.

Living Word of God,
live in our lives today.

Reflection

We are always more comfortable with 'people like us'. We naturally connect with people who share some of our values, culture and background. These bonds of trust and connection are called 'social capital', and such cohesion can be the mark of a healthy community. But many communities are now very divided; multiculturalism and migration have brought new challenges. The most valuable tool of social cohesion is called 'bridge-building social capital', when we find ways to get to know and trust people who are very different from us. Churches are ideally placed to offer this gift. The Bible teaches us to 'welcome the stranger', to break down the barriers between 'rich and poor, Jew and Gentile, slave and free', because in Christ we are all one. At the heart of our faith is a calling to value our diversity and so to find the deeper unity we share as children of God.

Let's take some time to reflect on our relationship as Christian churches.

Silence *(two minutes)*

In the silence we hold these questions:

How real is our unity?
How do we deal with our differences?
How do we demonstrate our unity to a divided world?
How do we relate to people of other faiths?

Music for Reflection – *suggestion*

Goodness of God, Jenn Johnson

Prayers of Recognition

Where we have been divided by inequality, social class, culture
and religion,
(Silence)

bring us together
in your mosaic of love.

Where we have been divided by prejudice, schism, disagreements
and dogma,
(Silence)

bring us together
in your mosaic of love.

Where we are called to be one in our shared mission to our
neighbourhood,
(Silence)

bring us together
in your mosaic of love.

Action

We now come to use the broken fragments that people have brought
with them to assemble a mosaic picture. We work together to make
a mosaic to express our commitment to Christian unity, and to that
deeper unity that spans all nations, cultures, religions and beliefs. We
use the broken fragments of the past to build a new future.

Music – *suggestion*

Goodness of God, Jenn Johnson

The Peace

When they were satisfied, Jesus told his disciples, 'Gather up the
fragments left over, so that nothing may be lost.'
John 6.12

May we be gathered and remade in the mosaic of God's love
and peace.

The peace of the Lord be always with you!
And also with you!

We share a sign of peace and unity.

Hymn – *suggestions*

Bind us together, Bob Gillman

Put peace into each other's hands, Fred Kaan

Prayers of Intercession

For this community of neighbours and strangers,
for those who have always lived here, and for those who are
newly arrived,
that we may learn to understand and trust one another:
(Silence)

bind us together, Lord,
with cords that cannot be broken.

For all local Christian churches, chapels, schools, projects
and networks,
that we may learn to appreciate our diversity and to work together:
(Silence)

bind us together, Lord,
with cords that cannot be broken.

For members of other faith groups who live or meet locally,
that we may learn to respect one another
and cherish common values:
(Silence)

bind us together, Lord,
with cords that cannot be broken.

For the gift of unity that you long to model in us,
for the practice of forgiveness and reconciliation
that we are called to share:
(Silence)

bind us together, Lord,
with cords that cannot be broken.

For the blessing of peace, for the sharing of wisdom,
for the growing in mission,
that you promise as we work and pray together:
(Silence)

bind us together, Lord,
with cords that cannot be broken.

Hymn – *suggestions*

We have a dream, Michael Forster

Jesus put this song into our hearts, Graham Kendrick

Blessing

God, who is love,
you see through our brokenness,
through our divisions and separation.
You long for us to be made whole.
Jesus, who is the human face of love,
you call us to gather the fragments,
so that nothing be lost.
You long for us to be healed.
Holy Spirit, who is the bond of love,
you build bridges of understanding and respect,
and break down the barriers that divide.
Father, Son and Holy Spirit,
bless us as we become your mosaic of love for the world.
Amen.

FEBRUARY

Kindled Light

Candlemas – lantern festival in the darkest part of the year

Preparation and Invitation

You will need enough sheets of coloured A4 thin card for each person to create a lantern. You will also need pairs of scissors to share, and sticky tape to secure the lanterns. You will need to provide battery-powered tealights for each lantern.

Gathering Music – *suggestion*

Nunc dimittis, Geoffrey Burgon

Welcome and Introduction

In the darkest part of the year, we celebrate the Feast of Candlemas, the Presentation of Christ in the Temple. When Joseph and Mary brought their tiny child to the Temple to 'do what was customary', they were greeted by Simeon, who took the child into his arms and gave thanks, calling Jesus 'a light for revelation to the Gentiles'. The prayerful elderly Anna also recognized the hope this baby represented for all seeking God's light. Today we shall explore what the darkness means for each of us, and for our world, and ask where we can find the light shining.

Hymn/Song – *suggestions*

Great is the darkness, Noel Richards

Hail, gladdening light, tr. John Keble

Opening Psalm

Where can I go from your spirit?
Or where can I flee from your presence?
If I ascend to heaven, you are there;
if I make my bed in Sheol, you are there.
If I take the wings of the morning
and settle at the farthest limits of the sea,
even there your hand shall lead me,
and your right hand shall hold me fast.
If I say, 'Surely the darkness shall cover me,
and the light around me become night',
even the darkness is not dark to you;
the night is as bright as the day,
for darkness is as light to you.
Psalm 139.7–12

Reading – *Desmond Tutu, Archbishop of Cape Town*

Hope is being able to see that there is light despite all of the darkness.
You see it wonderfully when you fly, and the sky is overcast. Sometimes you forget that, just beyond the clouds, the sun is shining.

Reflection

When do we stop worrying about our children? Desmond Tutu was
being interviewed in the *New York Times* and had been asked about
his son who is an alcoholic and had been arrested and imprisoned
for an attempted bombing. He replied with the words we have just
heard: words of hope not just for his own son but for all caught up in
violence, addiction or any kind of brooding darkness. When the world
seems overwhelmingly dark, can we still hope in the light? Desmond
Tutu's words can give us all hope.

Hymn/Song – *suggestion*

Goodness is stronger than evil, Desmond Tutu and John L. Bell

Bible Reading – *Luke 2.22–35*

When the time came for their purification according to the law of
Moses, they brought him up to Jerusalem to present him to the Lord

(as it is written in the law of the Lord, 'Every firstborn male shall be designated as holy to the Lord'), and they offered a sacrifice according to what is stated in the law of the Lord, 'a pair of turtle-doves or two young pigeons.'

Now there was a man in Jerusalem whose name was Simeon; this man was righteous and devout, looking forward to the consolation of Israel, and the Holy Spirit rested on him. It had been revealed to him by the Holy Spirit that he would not see death before he had seen the Lord's Messiah. Guided by the Spirit, Simeon came into the temple; and when the parents brought in the child Jesus, to do for him what was customary under the law, Simeon took him in his arms and praised God, saying,

Everyone says together:
'Master, now you are dismissing your servant in peace, according to your word;
for my eyes have seen your salvation,
which you have prepared in the presence of all peoples,
a light for revelation to the Gentiles
and for glory to your people Israel.'

The reader continues:
And the child's father and mother were amazed at what was being said about him. Then Simeon blessed them and said to his mother Mary, 'This child is destined for the falling and the rising of many in Israel, and to be a sign that will be opposed so that the inner thoughts of many will be revealed – and a sword will pierce your own soul too.'

Living Word of God,
live in our lives today.

Reflection

For Mary and Joseph, the birth of a child had been far from easy: conceived in scandal, no room for his birth at the inn, and later escaping into exile. Yet somehow all this had been held in the hope of God's promise that this would be no ordinary child. For Simeon, a lifetime of faithful hoping and waiting was suddenly fulfilled in this unlikely little family, as he recognized this child who would be 'a light for revelation to the Gentiles'.

Facing the darkness and yet still daring to affirm the light is something we are all called to do. It is easy to get overwhelmed watching the news or facing problems at home. Family and relationship worries, work issues, money and debt challenges, illness and poor health can all crowd in on us. We are tempted to look away, to close our eyes, but it helps us if we name and face the darkness. Equally, it can sometimes be hard to see any glimmer of light, any glimpse of hope in the darkness, but we are called to keep looking.

Silence *(two minutes)*

In the silence we hold these questions:

What is the darkness I am facing today, in my personal life and the life of the world?
Can I see any glimmers of light and hope?

Prayers of Recognition

We bring to God the darkness that we are facing in our personal lives,
all that obscures our way,
all that weighs heavy on our hearts and minds,
all that we cannot see beyond.
(Silence)

The light shines in the darkness,
and the darkness did not overcome it.
John 1.5

We bring to God the darkness that we are facing in the world
　around us,
all that makes us fearful,
all that threatens our well-being and survival,
all that we cannot see a way through.
(Silence)

The light shines in the darkness,
and the darkness did not overcome it.

We bring to God the light we can glimpse in our own experience,
moments of human kindness and love,
words of faith and hope that connect for us,
giving light for our next step.
(Silence)

The light shines in the darkness,
and the darkness did not overcome it.

We bring to God the light we can glimpse in the world around us,
people and movements that inspire us,
examples of reconciliation and forgiveness,
stories of good news.
(Silence)

The light shines in the darkness,
and the darkness did not overcome it.

Action

We choose a sheet of coloured card and share scissors and sticky tape
as we make a lantern for Candlemas.

1 Holding the card in portrait format, cut a strip about one
   centimetre wide along the top. Keep this to make the handle.
2 Fold the remaining card in half lengthways, then make a series of
   parallel cuts from the folded edge, about halfway into the card.
3 Unfold, then write on the strips making up the lantern opening the
   names of situations you would like to pray for later in the service.
4 Turn the card to landscape format, then bend it round to make a
   cylinder with the shorter edges just overlapping. Stick in place with
   tape, top and bottom.
5 Take a battery tealight and tape it into the bottom of the lantern.
6 Tape the handle strip to the top.

Music – *suggestion*

All-Night Vigil – Nunc dimittis, Sergei Rachmaninoff, sung by
Katie Melua

Hymn/Song – *suggestions*

The candle song (Like a candle flame), Graham Kendrick

Shine Jesus shine (Lord, the light of your love is shining),
Graham Kendrick

Prayers of Intercession

We take our lanterns of light and hope and hold them, extinguishing the main lighting in the worship space, to rely on the lantern light alone.

We pray for all new parents, like Mary and Joseph,
especially those facing dangers and fears,
that they may find welcome and support,
affirmation and care.
(Silence)

Jesus said, I am the light of the world.
No follower of mine shall wander in the dark,
but shall have the light of life.

We pray for older people, like Simeon and Anna,
especially those who live with infirmity and dementia,
that they may find understanding and compassion,
support and care.
(Silence)

No follower of mine shall wander in the dark,
but shall have the light of life.

We pray for all who struggle with the darkness of poor mental health,
stress, anxiety, depression, eating disorders, psychoses,
that they may find they are listened to, understood,
respected and embraced.
(Silence)

No follower of mine shall wander in the dark,
but shall have the light of life.

We pray for all who live with less than they need,
for all living in poverty, in poor housing or without a home,
that they may be noticed and helped,
shown their true worth.
(Silence)

No follower of mine shall wander in the dark,
but shall have the light of life.

We remember in silence the names and situations written on
    our lanterns,
held now in the light of God's love.
(Silence)

No follower of mine shall wander in the dark,
but shall have the light of life.

We remember those who have inspired us,
those who have faced the darkness and yet waited for the light,
those who have passed through death to life.
(Silence)

No follower of mine shall wander in the dark,
but shall have the light of life.

Hymn/Song – *suggestions*

Light of the world, Tim Hughes

Longing for light (Christ, be our light), Bernadette Farrell

Blessing

Creator God,
you spoke light into being,
light to shine in the darkness,
light to bring life to the universe.
Light of the world,
you came as one of us,
to face the deepest darkness,
light to bring hope to all people.
Inner light, Holy Spirit,
you come to show us the way,
to lighten our darkness,
to show us our next step.
Bless us now, Father, Son and Holy Spirit,
to live by your eternal light.
Amen.

Seven Whole Days

George Herbert – Sharing a faith for every day

Preparation and Invitation

This service takes the form of a pilgrimage around the inside of a church, with the congregation moving from station to station. You may need to make provision for people who are less mobile by placing chairs at various points, or it might be possible to remain in one place and to turn to the different stations. You may like to have a candle placed at each point of focus and light it as the station is reached in the service. You will need to provide enough votive candles or tealights for everyone to light one as part of their intercession.

You may like to reach out to a local book club, poetry reading group or college, and invite those who might be interested in George Herbert to act as readers of literature or poetry in the service. Another opportunity would be to invite a local history group who could add some particular insight into the features of your local church, perhaps speaking at each station.

Gathering Music – *we gather at the door to church – suggestion*

Let all the world in every corner sing, William Walton

Welcome and Introduction

Today we celebrate the life and spirituality of George Herbert: poet, musician, writer and above all parish priest, who showed us 'heaven in ordinary', how to live our Christian faith in our everyday lives, often through simple practical acts of care. Today we share in a pilgrimage around our church, pausing to understand the gift of this place and to reflect on how it connects with our journey through life. We begin here at the door.

Station 1 – The Door

Jesus said, 'I am the gate for the sheep.' He said, 'I came that they may have life and have it abundantly' (John 10.7, 10). That is what we are here for too, that all may find life, abundant life! The door, the threshold of our church, is meant to be open to welcome pilgrims and strangers. Everyone is welcome here!

Opening Responses

Jesus said, 'I am the good shepherd.
The good shepherd lays down his life for the sheep.
I am the good shepherd.
I know my own and my own know me,
just as the Father knows me and I know the Father.
And I lay down my life for the sheep.
John 10.11, 14–15

Hymn – *as we move to the next station – suggestion*

We love the place, O God, William Bullock and Henry Williams Baker

Station 2 – The Font

Jesus said, 'Come to me, all you that are weary and are carrying heavy burdens, and I will give you rest' (in other translations, 'refresh you') (Matthew 11.28). Often the font is to be found by the door to the church as baptism represents the way into the Christian faith, a fresh start on our life's pilgrimage. It may be that when we come to worship, to make a fresh start we need to lay down some of the heavy burdens we have been carrying. Burdens of regret and sorrow, of memories and mistakes. George Herbert said, 'Light burdens, long borne, grow heavy.' So we come to God to lay down our burdens in our prayers of recognition.

Prayers of Recognition

We bring to God all that we are carrying, the burdens we have
    been bearing.
We bring our painful memories,
we bring the times we have been hurt,
and we lay them down.
(Silence)

Jesus says, 'Come to me and I will refresh you.'
Lord, have mercy.

We bring to God all that we regret, the mistakes we have made,
the hurts we have caused.
We bring the times we have disappointed ourselves.
(Silence)

Jesus says, 'Come to me and I will refresh you.'
Christ, have mercy.

We bring to God all that we would change in our lives:
the sin that clings so closely,
the behaviours and attitudes that are unloving,
and our failure to listen to the Good Shepherd who leads us.
(Silence)

Jesus says, 'Come to me and I will refresh you.'
Lord, have mercy.

Assurance of Forgiveness

God of all goodness, slow to anger, quick to forgive,
as we lay down our burdens of regret,
as we let go of painful memories,
as we turn towards the light of your love,
give us grace to walk on with renewed strength,
to be changed into your likeness.
In Jesus' name we pray. **Amen.**

We each dip a finger into the font and make the sign of the cross on our
forehead to remember our baptism, the assurance of our sins forgiven.

Hymn – *as we move to the next station – suggestion*

The God of love my shepherd is, George Herbert

Station 3 – The Altar

Jesus said, 'Do this in remembrance of me' (Luke 22.19). From earliest
times, the heart of our worship is to be found in the breaking of bread
and the sharing of wine. The Eucharist feeds us, nurtures us, strength-
ens us for the journey. Here, as bread is broken, we hold all who are
broken, and we carry the hospitality of this table out into our daily
lives. This sacramental sharing embraces the whole of creation. 'Even
the swallow finds a nest for herself, where she may lay her young, at
your altars.' We join in the words of Psalm 84.

Psalm

How lovely is your dwelling place, O Lord of hosts!
My soul longs, indeed it faints for the courts of the Lord;
my heart and my flesh sing for joy to the living God.

Even the sparrow finds a home, and the swallow a nest for herself,
where she may lay her young, at your altars,
O Lord of hosts, my King and my God.
Happy are those who live in your house,
ever singing your praise.
Happy are those whose strength is in you,
in whose heart are the highways to Zion.
As they go through the valley of Baca they make it a place of springs;
the early rain also covers it with pools.
They go from strength to strength;
the God of gods will be seen in Zion.
O Lord God of hosts, hear my Prayer;
give ear, O God of Jacob!
Behold our shield, O God;
look on the face of your anointed.
For a day in your courts is better than a thousand elsewhere.
I would rather be a doorkeeper in the house of my God
than live in the tents of wickedness.
For the Lord God is a sun and shield;
he bestows favour and honour.
No good thing does the Lord withhold from those who
    walk uprightly.
O Lord of hosts, happy is everyone who trusts in you.

Glory to the Father and to the Son and to the Holy Spirit;
as it was in the beginning, is now and shall be for ever. Amen.
Psalm 84

Hymn – *as we move to the next station – suggestion*

Let all the world in every corner sing, George Herbert

Station 4 – Between the Lectern and Pulpit

Jesus said, 'Everyone then who hears these words of mine and acts on them will be like a wise man who built his house on rock' (Matthew 7.24). We stand between the lectern and the pulpit, between the reading of the word of God and the teaching of the Church. This is a place of listening, a place of dialogue, a place of wrestling. It is where we seek a faith that we can live by, a practical faith that makes a difference in our world. Listen now as God speaks to us through his living word.

Bible Reading – *Luke 11.5–10*

And Jesus said to them, 'Suppose one of you has a friend, and you go to him at midnight and say to him, "Friend, lend me three loaves of bread; for a friend of mine has arrived, and I have nothing to set before him." And he answers from within, "Do not bother me; the door has already been locked, and my children are with me in bed; I cannot get up and give you anything." I tell you, even though he will not get up and give him anything because he is his friend, at least because of his persistence he will get up and give him whatever he needs.

'So I say to you, Ask, and it will be given you; search, and you will find; knock, and the door will be opened for you. For everyone who asks receives, and everyone who searches finds, and for everyone who knocks, the door will be opened.'

Living Word of God,
live in our lives today.

Reflection

George Herbert was feted by kings and the royal court; he was destined for a career in politics but chose instead the life of a parish priest of two villages near Salisbury in Wiltshire. He wanted people to know that faith was something that could be found in our everyday living just as much as in church. It is essentially simple and practical, like getting up to give a neighbour some bread or a cup of water. It came from his sense that faith can imbue everything with value, that everything is sacred. Even sweeping a room, the most menial of tasks, can be transformed if it is done 'for thy sake'. His ministry was both prayerful and practical, bringing the sacrament to strengthen those who were ill at home, and food and clothing to those who were in need. We sing his words in the hymn, 'Teach me, my God and King'.

Hymn – *as we move to the next station – suggestion*

Teach me, my God and King, George Herbert

Station 5 – The Paschal Candle

Jesus said, 'Where two or three are gathered in my name, I am there among them' (Matthew 18.20). We come to a place of prayer where we hold the needs of the world and one another in the stream of God's grace. George Herbert called prayer 'the Christian plummet, sounding heaven and earth'. It is an invitation into the deep water of silence, into the uncharted territory of our deepest selves. In prayer we tune in to the 'cantus firmus', the 'enduring melody' of God's heartbeat of love. In prayer we do not need to convince God of our requests; God already knows and loves us completely. In our prayer we seek to tune our wills with God's will, to allow God's healing grace to flow through us.

Reading – *'Prayer (I)', George Herbert*

Prayer the church's banquet, angel's age,
God's breath in man returning to his birth,
The soul in paraphrase, heart in pilgrimage,
The Christian plummet sounding heav'n and earth;
Engine against th' Almighty, sinner's tow'r,
Reversed thunder, Christ-side-piercing spear,
The six-days world transposing in an hour,
A kind of tune, which all things hear and fear;
Softness, and peace, and joy, and love, and bliss,
Exalted manna, gladness of the best,
Heaven in ordinary, man well drest,

The milky way, the bird of Paradise,
Church-bells beyond the stars heard, the soul's blood,
The land of spices; something understood.

Our prayers link earth and heaven as we each come forward to light
a candle to represent a person or a concern that we would hold in the
heart of God's love. After all the candles have been lit, we pray:

Prayers of Intercession

Gracious God, hear now the deepest prayers of our hearts.
Bless and protect all who are cherished in these candle flames:
those who are unwell or unhappy,
those who are lonely or depressed, anxious or afraid,
those who are struggling with memory loss or dementia,
and those we name in the silence of our own hearts.
(Silence)

Let all the world in every corner sing,
my God and King!

God of our pilgrimage, bless now our church, set in this community.
May we be living stones, built into a holy temple to your glory,
whose faith finds expression in our daily lives,
through practical acts of generosity and care,
for all who are in need today.
(Silence)

Let all the world in every corner sing,
my God and King!

God of our belonging, thank you for calling us to be present in
    this place.
May we continue to bear witness to your presence,
at the heart of our community,
in moments of celebration and of deep sadness.
We pray for all who come to this place to mark the staging points on
    their life's journey.
(Silence)

Let all the world in every corner sing,
my God and King!

God of our inspiring, thank you for the beauty of this
    church building,
for the skill of the builders, the craftsmanship, the creativity,
for faith expressed in stone and wood, in fabric and flowers,
and in organ and voices filling the space with praise.
We pray for all who visit here, to find a moment of peace.
(Silence)

Let all the world in every corner sing,
my God and King!

God of eternity, you speak to us of heaven,
in the imagery of stained glass, of saints and angels praising you,
in the memory of past lives, carved in stone,
and in the echo of faithful prayer offered in this place
    over generations.
We pray for all who mourn today.
(Silence)

Let all the world in every corner sing,
my God and King!

We say together the prayer that Jesus taught us:

Our Father, who art in heaven,
hallowed be thy name;
thy kingdom come;
thy will be done;
on earth as it is in heaven.
Give us this day our daily bread.
And forgive us our trespasses,
as we forgive those who trespass against us.
And lead us not into temptation;
but deliver us from evil.
For thine is the kingdom,
the power and the glory,
for ever and ever.
Amen.

Hymn/Song – *as we move to the next station – suggestion*

King of glory, King of peace, George Herbert

Station 6 – The Door

Jesus said, 'Go into all the world and proclaim the good news to the whole creation' (Mark 16.15). So we come full circle as we return to the church door. The purpose of our gathering here, the purpose of our church, is to go out with good news on our lips and expressed in our lives. Good news to the people we live with, our neighbours, our work colleagues, good news to our community, to friend and stranger, good news to the whole creation! If we dare to allow it, our faith will change our way of living, our way of relating, even the impact we have on our planet. So we commit to be people of God's good news, seven whole days, not one in seven!

Act of Commitment

We commit to being people of prayer,
seeking God in stillness and silence,
holding others in the stream of God's grace.
(Silence)

Seven whole days, not one in seven,
I will praise thee.

We commit to being people of action,
looking for opportunities to care for family and friends,
to care for neighbours and strangers,
transforming our community life together.
(Silence)

Seven whole days, not one in seven,
I will praise thee.

We commit to being changed by our faith,
to live more sustainably, to waste less and to recycle more,
to care for our environment, and to protect our climate,
to be good stewards of creation.
(Silence)

Seven whole days, not one in seven,
I will praise thee.

Blessing

Go forth into the world in peace.
The Lord keep you from all evil; he will keep your life.
The Lord keep your going out and your coming in,
from this time on and for evermore.
May the blessing of God, Father, Son and Holy Spirit
be with you and remain with you,
seven whole days, not one in seven.
Amen.

MARCH

On the Level

St Chad – Celtic liturgy and
pilgrimage prayer walk

Preparation and Invitation

You will need to devise a suitable route for a pilgrimage walk, passing and pausing at various places to pray. You can make it a circular walk beginning and ending in church, or if you have two possible venues you might like to start in church and finish in a community space. Review the service for the possible prayer stations that could be planned.

Invite different members of the church or wider community to lead a section of the walk that connects with their life or interests.

Refreshments can be a good way to end this pilgrimage: breaking bread and sharing homemade soup, or a 'bring and share' picnic.

Gathering Music – *suggestion*

Who would true valour see, Maddy Prior and the Carnival Band

Welcome and Introduction

Today we celebrate St Chad, one of our earliest Celtic saints, of the seventh century. When Columba brought the good news to the Scottish island of Iona and established a monastery, he trained monks and sent them out as missionaries. He sent Aidan to Lindisfarne, who called and trained Chad to be a missionary too. Chad was recognized for his gifts and appointed bishop of the Northumbrians, but when a conflict arose about the validity of his appointment he humbly stepped down. Later he was appointed bishop of the Mercians, and established the centre of the diocese at Lichfield. There is a story of Chad being presented with a horse to help him to travel around more effectively, but he gave the horse away to someone who needed it more than him. He preferred to walk, to be on the level with his people, to meet them face to face, to look them in the eye. Today we will follow his example, following Christ in the footsteps of St Chad.

Hymn/Song – *suggestions*

He who would valiant be, John Bunyan, Percy Dearmer

One more step along the road I go, Sydney Carter

Opening Psalm

Happy are the people who know the festal shout,
who walk, O Lord, in the light of your countenance;
they exult in your name all day long,
and extol your righteousness.
For you are the glory of their strength;
by your favour our horn is exalted.
For our shield belongs to the Lord,
our king to the Holy One of Israel.
Psalm 89.15–18

Bible Reading – *Luke 10.1–6*

After this the Lord appointed seventy others and sent them on ahead of him in pairs to every town and place where he himself intended to go. He said to them, 'The harvest is plentiful, but the labourers are few; therefore ask the Lord of the harvest to send out labourers into his harvest. Go on your way. See, I am sending you out like lambs into the midst of wolves. Carry no purse, no bag, no sandals; and greet no one on the road. Whatever house you enter, first say, "Peace to this house!" And if anyone is there who shares in peace, your peace will rest on that person; but if not, it will return to you.'

Living Word of God,
live in our lives today.

Reflection

Often we think about being a Christian in terms of coming to church. We have become a static people. We think of mission in terms of attracting other people to 'come to church', and much of our church life is geared around these assumptions. But Jesus spent most of his ministry going to where the people were, to the market, the lakeside, and he sent out his disciples in pairs to all of the communities around. Our short time together as 'gathered church' is really intended to equip us for the much more extensive part of our life as 'scattered church' in the mission of our everyday lives.

Silence *(two minutes)*

In the silence we hold these questions:

Where will we each be this time tomorrow?

Where do we encounter people in our local community and in our daily lives?

Conversation

We turn to our neighbour, identifying the places where we personally are 'scattered church' and the opportunities this gives us to bear witness to our faith.

Prayer

God of our pilgrimage,
give us grace to walk with you
through the highways and byways of our community.
Help us to recognize you, present in our world
and in the faces of those we meet on the way.
May we follow Christ in the footsteps of St Chad.
Amen.

Action

In our pilgrimage today we walk with Jesus and the disciples to recognize God at work in the world around us.

Song – *suggestion*

We walk his way, South African, tr. Anders Nyberg and Sven-
Bernhard Fast

A Farm/Field/Allotment

We think of the land, our farms and farmers.
We think of the changing patterns of farming, of mechanization.
We think of the impact of our farming on the climate and
environment.

Reading – *Genesis 2.8–9*

> And the Lord God planted a garden in Eden, in the east; and there
> he put the man whom he had formed. Out of the ground the Lord
> God made to grow every tree that is pleasant to the sight and good
> for food, the tree of life also in the midst of the garden, and the tree
> of the knowledge of good and evil.

Living Word of God,
live in our lives today.

Reflection

The Bible tells of God in creation giving us a fruitful garden world
and calling us to till and farm it. We are called to be good stewards of
creation, but we have abused the earth, taking without care, wasting
without heed of the consequences. Now, as we recognize the consequences of our greed, we face a climate crisis, pollution, species loss
and a growing awareness that we will need to change. We think of
our farms and farmers in these challenging times. How do we need to
change the way we are living?

Thanksgiving

For the fertility of the land and the work of our farmers,
we give you thanks, O God.

For the subtle balance of nature and the diversity of all life,
we give you thanks, O God.
For the fields that produce food, the harvest of our land,
we give you thanks, O God.

Prayer

God of all creation,
give us wisdom to use your gifts well,
to understand the impact of our farming.
Give us courage to act in the face of climate change,
give us generous hearts to share with those who go hungry,
as we follow Christ in the footsteps of St Chad.
Amen.

Business and Retail Life

We think of our business life, of manufacturing, sales and services.
We think of our economy, of profit and loss.
We think of jobs and income.

Bible Reading – *Amos 8.4–6*

> Hear this, you that trample on the needy,
> and bring to ruin the poor of the land,
> saying, 'When will the new moon be over
> so that we may sell grain;
> and the sabbath,
> so that we may offer wheat for sale?
> We will make the ephah small and the shekel great,
> and practise deceit with false balances,
> buying the poor for silver and the needy for a pair of sandals,
> and selling the sweepings of the wheat.'

Living Word of God,
live in our lives today.

Reflection

The people of Israel developed a strong work ethic and reputation for trade and business. But the Bible repeatedly warns that trade must be fair, that businesses must be run within a strong ethical framework. The prophet Amos warns about trampling the needy and 'buying the poor for silver'. Our demand for ever lower prices can lead to just that: low wages, poor returns, and exploitation of those who have the least in society. How do we need to change if we are to be faithful in business?

Thanksgiving

For entrepreneurs and people in business who innovate new products
    and services,
we give you thanks, O God.
For good employers who offer fair pay and steady jobs,
we give you thanks, O God.
For honest dealing and justice in world trade,
we give you thanks, O God.

Prayer

God of enterprise and opportunity,
give us the imagination and creativity to do good business.
In all our dealings help us to be honest and fair,
respecting suppliers, employees and customers,
conserving the resources of the earth and acting sustainably,
as we follow Christ in the footsteps of St Chad.
Amen.

Sign Post

We think of the turning points in our lives.
We think of the decisions we are facing, the choices we need to make.
We think of the changes we have seen in our community.

Bible Reading – *Jeremiah 31.21–25*

Set up road markers for yourself, make yourself signposts; consider well the highway, the road by which you went. Return, O virgin Israel, return to these your cities. How long will you waver, O faithless daughter?

Thus says the Lord of hosts, the God of Israel: Once more they shall use these words in the land of Judah and in its towns when I restore their fortunes: 'The Lord bless you, O abode of righteousness, O holy hill!' And Judah and all its towns shall live there together, and the farmers and those who wander with their flocks. I will satisfy the weary, and all who are faint I will replenish.

Living Word of God,
live in our lives today.

Reflection

God calls us to reflect on the journey we have made in our lives, to think about the turning points and decisions we have taken. Sometimes we have made poor choices and lost our way. Like the people of Israel, we sometimes feel far from home, in exile. But Jeremiah promises that God will restore his people. There are no dead ends with God. The question is always: where do we go from here?

Thanksgiving

For the times we have lost our sense of direction but found a new way,
we give you thanks, O God.
For the turning points and opportunities to choose a responsible way,
we give you thanks, O God.
For those we have met on our journey who have guided us on our way,
we give you thanks, O God.

Prayer

God of our pilgrimage,
with us every step of the way,
help us to recognize the turning points and diversions on our path,
and to find our sense of direction and purpose,
as we follow Christ in the footsteps of St Chad.
Amen.

Pub/Café

We think of the gift of hospitality, of refreshment of shared meals.
We think of the people Jesus chose to eat with, of breaking bread
   with strangers.
We think of the food we eat, and of those who will go hungry.

Bible Reading – *Luke 24.28–32*

As they came near the village to which they were going, he walked
ahead as if he were going on. But they urged him strongly, saying,
'Stay with us, because it is almost evening and the day is now nearly
over.' So he went in to stay with them. When he was at the table with
them, he took bread, blessed and broke it, and gave it to them. Then
their eyes were opened, and they recognized him; and he vanished
from their sight. They said to each other, 'Were not our hearts burning within us while he was talking to us on the road, while he was
opening the scriptures to us?'

Living Word of God,
live in our lives today.

Reflection

Two disciples walking home, heads hung low with loss and grief, meet
a stranger on the road who seems to know all about them, but it is only
when they invite him to stay for a meal that they recognize Jesus in the
breaking of the bread. The gift of hospitality is central to our Christian
faith. It is how we meet Jesus today. We are quite good at sharing food
with friends and family, but can we extend our circle?

Thanksgiving

For all places of hospitality and welcome in our community,
we give you thanks, O God.
For opportunities to include strangers and to break bread with them,
we give you thanks, O God.

For entertaining angels unawares,
we give you thanks, O God.

Prayer

God of unexpected encounters,
we thank you for times we have found refreshment and welcome.
Meet us in our sharing of hospitality,
surprise us with your blessing,
as we follow Christ in the footsteps of St Chad.
Amen.

Park/Play Area

We think of times of rest and recreation in our lives.
We think of the balance of work and play, of giving and receiving.
We think of the children in our community, and of the child in
    each of us.

Bible Reading – *Matthew 18.1–5*

At that time the disciples came to Jesus and asked, 'Who is the greatest in the kingdom of heaven?' He called a child, whom he put among them, and said, 'Truly I tell you, unless you change and become like children, you will never enter the kingdom of heaven. Whoever becomes humble like this child is the greatest in the kingdom of heaven. Whoever welcomes one such child in my name welcomes me.'

Living Word of God,
live in our lives today.

Reflection

When did you last play a game? When did you last play with children, entering their amazing world of imagination? Each of us was once a child, and that inner child is still part of us. Of course we need to grow into a mature faith, yet Jesus said we need to 'change and become like children' if we want to enter the kingdom of heaven! Part of the balance of life for us will be between the serious grown-up world of work and responsibility, and the gift of space and time to rest, play and renew our deepest selves.

Thanksgiving

For space and time to rest and play,
we give you thanks, O God.
For the gift of children in our lives and communities, reminding us
of heaven,
we give you thanks, O God.
For the freedom and imagination to be our true selves,
we give you thanks, O God.

Prayer

God of rest and recreation, God of play and possibility,
help us to make time in our lives to rediscover the child still within us.
Where we have become overburdened with responsibility,
show us how to change and become like children again,
trusting and free in the safety of your love,
as we follow Christ in the footsteps of St Chad.
Amen.

School/Nursery

We think of our education and the opportunities we have for learning.
We think of someone who was an influential teacher in our lives.
We think of someone who taught us about Jesus.

Bible Reading – *Luke 6.40, 46–49*

A disciple is not above the teacher, but everyone who is fully qual-
ified will be like the teacher. Why do you call me 'Lord, Lord', and
do not do what I tell you? I will show you what someone is like who
comes to me, hears my words, and acts on them. That one is like a
man building a house, who dug deeply and laid the foundation on
rock; when a flood arose, the river burst against that house but could

not shake it, because it had been well built. But the one who hears and does not act is like a man who built a house on the ground without a foundation. When the river burst against it, immediately it fell, and great was the ruin of that house.

Living Word of God,
live in our lives today.

Reflection

What is education for? How do we measure the performance of our schools and colleges? Is it all about examination results and qualifications? It is easy for some subjects to get left behind when the pressure is on. Is there room for music, art, drama, for faith to be explored? What does it mean to 'dig deeply' and to 'lay the foundation on rock'? What is it that builds real resilience, to help us to withstand the storms and floods of life?

Thanksgiving

For good teachers who help us to dig deep and lay solid foundations,
we give you thanks, O God.
For nurseries, schools, colleges and adult education providers,
we give you thanks, O God.
For opportunities to continue our education throughout our life,
we give you thanks, O God.

Prayer

God of all learning and wisdom,
deepen our understanding,
widen our knowledge,
broaden our experience.
Help us to continue to grow and to learn,
throughout our lives,
to find your deep wisdom,
as the foundation for our living,
as we follow Christ in the footsteps of St Chad.
Amen.

Destination

We think of our whole community.
We think of our pilgrimage, following Christ in the footsteps of
St Chad.
We pledge to continue to serve and to pray for our community.

Bible Reading – *Jeremiah 29.11–14*

For surely I know the plans I have for you, says the Lord, plans for
your welfare and not for harm, to give you a future with hope. Then
when you call upon me and come and pray to me, I will hear you.
When you search for me, you will find me; if you seek me with all
your heart, I will let you find me, says the Lord, and I will restore
your fortunes and gather you from all the nations and all the places
where I have driven you, says the Lord, and I will bring you back to
the place from which I sent you into exile.

Living Word of God,
live in our lives today.

Reflection

God cares about the whole of our community, and we are called to
care too. God holds a vision for our community, of welfare, to give us
a future with hope. As we complete our pilgrimage, we pledge that we
will continue to pray for our community.

Thanksgiving

For all that is good in our community, signs of God's kingdom
among us,
we give you thanks, O God.
For all that is challenging in our community, signs of God's longing
for change,
we give you thanks, O God.

For all who live, work or travel through this place, each one a child of God,
we give you thanks, O God.

Final Prayer

God who plans for our whole community,
for our welfare and our future,
give us grace to meet people on the level,
to walk beside them, to look them in the eye,
to see in them your image and likeness,
as we follow Christ in the footsteps of St Chad.
Amen.

Blessing

God who calls us to walk the steep and rugged pathway,
Jesus who comes to journey beside us,
Spirit who awakens us to the saints along our way,
bless us now, and as we journey on.
Amen.

Simnel Share

Mothering Sunday – Gathering the fragments of family life

Preparation and Invitation

In this service each person attending will be given a small portion of the ingredients of a simnel cake, to be combined to make a cake together. You will need to set up a table with a large bowl and a mixing spoon. You will also need to ask some people to make simnel cakes to bring to the service to be shared at the end of the service. You may like to link with local groups that do baking as part of their regular activity, such as the Women's Institute or Mothers' Union, or a local college teaching food technology.

Recipes for simnel cake can be found online, for example: https:// britishfoodhistory.com/2018/03/19/simnel-cake/.

Gathering Music – *suggestion*

Hymn to the Mother of God, John Tavener

Welcome and Introduction

The fourth Sunday in Lent was traditionally a day of refreshment from the Lenten fast. People would return home to their 'mother' church, and often to their own mothers, to celebrate. Young people 'in service', working as domestic servants away from home, would be allowed to visit their family on this day. They would take with them a simnel cake to share. In our worship today we will be thinking about family life, its joys and its challenges, now sometimes more fractured than ever, about domestic service and migrant workers living apart from their families. We begin with our first hymn.

Hymn/Song – *suggestions*

Now thank we all our God, Martin Rinkart,
tr. Catherine Winkworth.

Take this moment, sign and space, John L. Bell

Opening Psalm

Happy is everyone who fears the Lord,
who walks in his ways.
You shall eat the fruit of the labour of your hands;
you shall be happy, and it shall go well with you.
Your wife will be like a fruitful vine
within your house;
your children will be like olive shoots
around your table.
Thus shall the man be blessed
who fears the Lord.
The Lord bless you from Zion.
May you see the prosperity of Jerusalem
all the days of your life.
May you see your children's children.
Peace be upon Israel!

Glory to the Father and to the Son and to the Holy Spirit;
as it was in the beginning, is now and shall be for ever. Amen.
Psalm 128

Reading – *'Mothering Sunday', Malcolm Guite*

At last, in spite of all, a recognition,
For those who loved and laboured for so long,
Who brought us, through that labour, to fruition
To flourish in the place where we belong.
A thanks to those who stayed and did the raising,

55

Who buckled down and did the work of two,
Whom governments have mocked instead of praising,
Who hid their heart-break and still struggled through,
The single mothers forced onto the edge
Whose work the world has overlooked, neglected,
Invisible to wealth and privilege,
But in whose lives the kingdom is reflected.
Now into Christ our mother church we bring them,
Who shares with them the birth-pangs of His Kingdom.

Reflection

The simnel cake tradition is thought to go back to the twelfth century and was a gift made from the finest flour. The recipe has taken many forms; today it is a fruit cake topped with marzipan with eleven small marzipan balls representing the disciples, not including Judas who betrayed Jesus. Malcolm Guite's wonderful sonnet for Mothering Sunday cuts through the sugary sweetness of some idealized pictures of mothering, to focus on the gritty reality of what it is to be a single mother. Many families today are fragmented in different ways, with the demands of work, different shift patterns, sometimes a long commute. There are pressures for families who have been divided by conflict, arguments, divorce, or for blended families where new patterns are needed. Even in the same house we can be fragmented by technology, each able to be on our own screens, follow our own interests, eating at different times. Perhaps we need Mothering Sunday even more than ever.

Hymn/Song – *suggestion*

God our creator, hear us sing in praise, Stephen Eric Smith

Here in this place, Marty Haugen

Bible Reading – *1 Kings 17.8–16*

Then the word of the Lord came to him, saying, 'Go now to Zarephath, which belongs to Sidon, and live there; for I have commanded a widow there to feed you.' So he set out and went to Zarephath. When he came to the gate of the town, a widow was there gathering sticks; he called to her and said, 'Bring me a little water in a vessel, so that I may drink.' As she was going to bring it, he called to her and said, 'Bring me a morsel of bread in your hand.' But she said, 'As the Lord your God lives, I have nothing baked, only a handful of meal in a jar, and a little oil in a jug; I am now gathering a couple of sticks, so that I may go home and prepare it for myself and my son, that we may eat it, and die.' Elijah said to her, 'Do not be afraid; go and do as you have said; but first make me a little cake of it and bring it to me, and afterwards make something for yourself and your son. For thus says the Lord the God of Israel: 'The jar of meal will not be emptied and the jug of oil will not fail until the day that the Lord sends rain on the earth.' She went and did as Elijah said, so that she as well as he and her household ate for many days. The jar of meal was not emptied, neither did the jug of oil fail, according to the word of the Lord that he spoke by Elijah.

Living Word of God,
live in our lives today.

Reflection

The widow of Zarephath had her own problems – she had enough on her plate! She had lost her husband, her provider and protector. She was struggling to provide for her son because of a drought that had led to famine. And here she is caught by the demands of hospitality: a stranger calls and asks for help. I wonder why she didn't send him away with a flea in his ear! Often it is the poorest who are the most generous. Her generosity is rewarded; and in a sign that would be repeated when Jesus fed the five thousand with nothing but five small loaves and two fish, her meagre supply of flour and oil is sufficient. God has a way of gathering the fragments and making them enough to meet our needs. When our family life is stretched to breaking point, when we feel we will run out of energy or patience or even of love, God can give us the resources we need – if we will let him. We will take a time to reflect, to think about where our family life is fractured or stretched.

Silence *(two minutes)*

In the silence we hold these questions:

What are the pressures I am facing in my life?
Where am I running out of resources?

Prayers of Recognition

We bring to God the pressures we face in our lives,
where our relationships are fragmented by the demands of life,
where we feel inadequate, not knowing how we will cope.
(Silence)

I have nothing –
do not be afraid.

We bring to God the demands that are made on us,
the expectations of others that we will provide for them,
where we feel empty, not knowing how we will cope.
(Silence)

I have nothing –
do not be afraid.

We bring to God the conflicts and divisions that sap our energy,
the arguments and disputes that consume us,
where we feel wrung out, not knowing how we will cope.
(Silence)

I have nothing –
do not be afraid.

Simnel Sharing

We bring forward the ingredients for a simnel cake, taking it in turns to add our fragments to the whole and to stir the mix, making it a prayerful action. We offer what we have, and pray that God will make it enough. After the service, the cake will be baked and shared with those unable to come to church.

Music – *suggestion*

Hymn to the Mother of God, John Tavener

Hymn/Song – *suggestion*

I am the bread of life, Suzanne Toolan

I heard the voice of Jesus say, Horatius Bonar

Prayers of Intercession

God, you long to gather us under your wings,
like a mother hen gathers her chicks.
Bless our family life,
that our homes may be peaceful,
places of welcome, love and security,
where we can grow to maturity,
in faith and trust.
(Silence)

Gather the fragments.
Make them whole.

God of every family under heaven,
bless all who are apart from their families at this time:
those who are employed as migrant workers,
those who are fleeing from war or persecution,
those caught up in modern slavery.
(Silence)

Gather the fragments.
Make them whole.

God of the widow of Zarephath,
bless all who are struggling to make ends meet:
those who are out of work, or unable to work,
those who are unsupported and vulnerable.
(Silence)

Gather the fragments.
Make them whole.

God of new patterns and possibilities,
bless all who are working to make new patterns of family life work:
those who are living in blended families,
those who have adopted or fostered children.
(Silence)

Gather the fragments.
Make them whole.

God who called Mary to be the mother of your son Jesus,
bless our own mothers today in their vocation.
Hold all who have longed to be mothers but not had the opportunity,
and those who are feeling overwhelmed by their responsibilities.
(Silence)

Gather the fragments.
Make them whole.

God of time and eternity,
bless all who mourn the death of their mother.
Hold all who have passed through death in your arms of love.
(Silence)

Gather the fragments.
Make them whole.

We pray the prayer that Jesus taught us:

Our Father, who art in heaven,
hallowed be thy name;
thy kingdom come;
thy will be done;
on earth as it is in heaven.
Give us this day our daily bread.
And forgive us our trespasses,
as we forgive those who trespass against us.
And lead us not into temptation;
but deliver us from evil.
For thine is the kingdom,
the power and the glory,
for ever and ever.
Amen.

Hymn/Song – *suggestions*

Tell out my soul, Timothy Dudley Smith

Lord, we thank you for the promise, Martin E. Leckebusch

Blessing

Mothering God,
like a mother hen you long to gather us
under the shadow and protection of your wing.
Where we are empty,
fill us with your love.
Where we are fragmented,
make us whole.
Where we are lost,
bring us home to you
to rejoice in the joy and fullness of your love
flowing among us and within us.
May the blessing of God, Father, Son and Holy Spirit,
be with us all, today and every day.
Amen.

Sharing Simnel Cake

We share refreshments and a slice of simnel cake.

APRIL

Harrowing and Hoping

Easter – Breaking through to new life in tough times

Preparation and Invitation

This service offers a different way of marking the Easter season. It is particularly suitable for people who have been bereaved, so you could specifically invite those who have lost loved ones. Sometimes the joy of Easter can be hard if you are grieving.

During the service people will be invited to sow some seeds. You will need plant pots, potting compost and seeds for everyone. Suitable seeds might be sunflower, runner bean or sweet pea, or a selection to give people a choice.

Gathering Music – *suggestion*

Blackbird, The Beatles

Welcome and Introduction

Easter is a time for sowing seeds! Every year we re-enact the story of Jesus' death and resurrection in our own gardens. For those who have been bereaved, our own grief and loss is mirrored in the same way, as we seek to break through the sadness of our hearts, to allow the seeds of hope to grow in us again. Today we ask God to harrow our hearts and to let the resurrection life grow in us.

Easter Acclamation

Alleluia, Christ is risen!
He is risen indeed, Alleluia!

Hymn/Song – *suggestions*

Now the green blade riseth, John Macleod Campbell Crum

Great is the darkness, Noel Richards

Opening Psalm

When the righteous cry for help, the Lord hears,
and rescues them from all their troubles.
The Lord is near to the broken-hearted,
and saves the crushed in spirit.
Many are the afflictions of the righteous,
but the Lord rescues them from them all.
He keeps all their bones;
not one of them will be broken.
Psalm 34.17–20

Opening Prayer

God of our living and of our dying,
God of our longing and of our hoping,
God who brings life out of death,
hold us now in the deep loam of your love.
Harrow our hearts, break us open to new possibilities,
to grow and live in your resurrection life,
through Jesus, who died, was buried and who rose again for us.
Amen.

Reflection

In medieval times the tradition of the 'harrowing of hell' was a popular theme: the belief that Jesus, once he was laid in the tomb, descended into hell to release all the imprisoned souls. The image of harrowing is so powerful. The farmer will harrow a field to break open the hardened lumps of earth, to create a fine tilth ready for seeds to germinate and break into new life. This reading is from *Piers Plowman* by William Langland, a narrative poem written in Middle English in around 1370–90.

Reading – *Piers Plowman*

The light commanded them to unlock, and Lucifer answered, 'Who is this? What lord are you?' Swiftly the light answered: 'The king of glory; the Lord of might and main and all virtues; the Lord of power. Dukes of this dim place, undo these gates at once, that Christ may enter, the King of heaven's Son!'

And with that breath hell broke open, and Belial's bars; no matter any guard or watchman, the gates opened wide. Patriarchs and prophets, the souls in darkness, sang St John's song: 'Behold the Lamb of God!' Lucifer could not look, he was so blinded by light. And those whom Our Lord loved he caught up into his light, and said to Satan:

'Lo, here is my soul to make amends for all sinful souls, to save those who are worthy. Mine they are, and of me, and so I may the better claim them … I will lead from here the people whom I loved and who believed in my coming.'

Hymn/Song – *suggestions*

This joyful Eastertide, George Ratcliffe Woodward

Dance and sing all the earth, John L. Bell and Graham Maule

Bible Reading – *Luke 24.1–12*

But on the first day of the week, at early dawn, they came to the tomb, taking the spices that they had prepared. They found the stone rolled away from the tomb, but when they went in, they did not find the body. While they were perplexed about this, suddenly two men in dazzling clothes stood beside them. The women were terrified and bowed their faces to the ground, but the men said to them, 'Why do you look for the living among the dead? He is not here, but has risen. Remember how he told you, while he was still in Galilee, that the Son of Man must be handed over to sinners, and be crucified, and on the third day rise again.' Then they remembered his words, and returning from the tomb, they told all this to the eleven and to all the rest. Now it was Mary Magdalene, Joanna, Mary the mother of James, and the other women with them who told this to the apostles.

But these words seemed to them an idle tale, and they did not believe them. But Peter got up and ran to the tomb; stooping and looking in, he saw the linen cloths by themselves; then he went home, amazed at what had happened.

Living Word of God,
live in our lives today.

Reflection

When someone you love dies, it is as though part of you has died too. Grief can be overwhelming and deadening. It sucks the life out of us. The women who went to the tomb and the disciples who did all that rushing about were just like us. Death is disorientating. Our hearts can become hardened by grief, we cannot imagine how we could ever live or laugh again. We need the risen Jesus to harrow our hearts, to let the green shoots of new life grow in us again – the seeds of hope.

Jesus was always good at asking 'harrowing' questions that would break us open. To Simon Peter who had denied him he said, 'Simon son of John, do you love me?' (John 21.17). He opened Simon to the possibility of reconciliation. To the man called Legion, possessed by evil spirits, he asked, 'What is your name?' (Luke 8.30). He opened him to the possibility of recovering his true identity. To the woman with a haemorrhage who touched him in a crowd, 'Who touched me?' (Luke 8.45). He opened her to the possibility of recognizing that it was her own faith that had healed her.

In this time of silence, we give space to listen for the harrowing question that God is asking us. What needs to be broken open in us for new life to grow?

Silence *(two minutes)*

In the silence we hold these questions:

What needs breaking open in my life?
What question is God asking me today?

Music for Reflection – *suggestion*

Goldberg Variations, BWV 988 – Aria, Johann Sebastian Bach

Prayers of Recognition

We bring to God our tentative hopes,
our longing for signs of new life,
our trust in God's creative goodness.
(Silence)

Harrow our hearts,
that we may live again.

We bring to God all that has hardened our hearts,
the pain and grief of losing someone we love,
the regrets and disappointments we have known.
(Silence)

Harrow our hearts,
that we may live again.

We bring to God all that has become fixed and immovable in us,
our routines and habits,
the ruts that we live in without thinking.
(Silence)

Harrow our hearts,
that we may live again.

We bring to God our entrenched positions,
the attitudes that we maintain without thinking,
the prejudices that we harbour.
(Silence)

Harrow our hearts,
that we may live again.

Action

As a continuation of our reflections we each fill a pot with compost, pausing to thank God for the loam of his love. Then we sow some seeds, perhaps sunflower, sweet pea or runner bean, picturing each one as an opening to new life for us. We take them home to germinate and to nurture.

Music – *suggestion*

Goldberg Variations, BWV 988 – Aria, Johann Sebastian Bach

Hymn/Song – *suggestions*

In the garden Mary lingers, Martin E. Leckebusch

Spirit divine, attend our prayers, Andrew Reed

Prayers of Intercession

We pray that the seeds of your Spirit will grow in us,
bringing forth the fruit of the Spirit,
a harvest of love, joy and peace.
(Silence)

God of new possibilities,
grow in our lives today.

We pray for the farmers and gardeners
preparing the earth for cultivation,
removing weeds and stones,
harrowing the soil to make ready for the seeds to grow.
(Silence)

God of new possibilities,
grow in our lives today.

We pray for all in business and commerce
who are preparing to launch new products,
to begin new ventures, hoping to create employment.
(Silence)

God of new possibilities,
grow in our lives today.

We pray for those beginning a new relationship,
those moving to a new home,
those hoping to start a family.
(Silence)

God of new possibilities,
grow in our lives today.

We pray for those wanting to make a change in their lives,
to live more sustainably,
to care for our environment.
(Silence)

God of new possibilities,
grow in our lives today.

We pray for all who are struggling with illness or disability,
all who have memory loss or dementia,
all who are grieving the death of a loved one.
(Silence)

God of new possibilities,
grow in our lives today.

We remember all who have died,
giving thanks for the life and love they shared.
Welcome them into your resurrection life,
and bring us all into your kingdom,
through Jesus Christ our Lord.
Amen.

Hymn/Song – *suggestions*

Oh the life of the world, Kathy Galloway

Alleluia! Alleluia! Hearts to heaven and voices raise,
Christopher Wordsworth

Blessing

God of Easter hope, hold us!
God of Easter joy, enfold us!
God of resurrection life, flow through us!
May the blessing of God, Father, Son and Holy Spirit,
Be with you, now and for ever.
Amen.

Night Watch

Lambing Sunday – Celebration of the Good Shepherd

Preparation and Invitation

The lambing season in the UK runs from March to May, so the timing of this service could come as a thanksgiving for the completion of lambing time. If there are any farms raising sheep in your area, or any shepherds working locally, you may like to contact them to invite them to attend or take part in the service. Sometimes we have been able to have some new lambs in church, which is always popular!

During the service people are invited to make a wool cross. You may be able to obtain some raw wool from the fields and fences, or to ask a farmer for some wool from shearing. You could use commercial spun wool as an alternative to raw wool. You will also need some cotton thread to secure the crosses.

Gathering Music – *suggestion*

Chasing sheep is best left to shepherds, Michael Nyman

Welcome and Introduction

Today we give thanks for our farming community and especially for all shepherds. When Jesus was born into our world, it was the shepherds who were summoned to be the first witnesses of his birth. In his adult life Jesus described himself as the good shepherd who lays down his life for the sheep. We are the sheep of his pasture, so let us worship him today.

Hymn/Song – *suggestions*

> The Lord's my shepherd, Stuart Townend
>
> The Lord's my shepherd (Brother James' Air), James Leith Macbeth Bain

Opening Psalm

O come, let us worship and bow down,
let us kneel before the Lord, our Maker!
For he is our God,
and we are the people of his pasture,
and the sheep of his hand.
Psalm 95.6–7

Reading – '*Young Lambs*', *John Clare*

> The spring is coming by a many signs;
> The trays are up, the hedges broken down,
> That fenced the haystack, and the remnant shines
> Like some old antique fragment weathered brown.
> And where suns peep, in every sheltered place,
> The little early buttercups unfold
> A glittering star or two – till many trace
> The edges of the blackthorn clumps in gold.
> And then a little lamb bolts up behind
> The hill and wags his tail to meet the yoe,
> And then another, sheltered from the wind,
> Lies all his length as dead – and lets me go
> Close bye and never stirs but baking lies,
> With legs stretched out as though he could not rise.

Bible Reading – *Isaiah 40.9–11*

Get you up to a high mountain,
O Zion, herald of good tidings;
lift up your voice with strength,
O Jerusalem, herald of good tidings,
lift it up, do not fear;
say to the cities of Judah,
'Here is your God!'
See, the Lord God comes with might,
and his arm rules for him;
his reward is with him,
and his recompense before him.
He will feed his flock like a shepherd;
he will gather the lambs in his arms,
and carry them in his bosom,
and gently lead the mother sheep.

Living Word of God,
live in our lives today.

Reflection

John Clare (1793–1864) was the son of a farm labourer, and in his poems he observed the rhythms and disruptions of farm life in the nineteenth century. His picture of young lambs would be recognizable in biblical times, as it is to this day.

What a contrast to the many war-like images of God in the Hebrew Scriptures! Here God is presented as a gentle shepherd, gathering the lambs into his arms. Shepherding takes patience and endurance, even today, and lambing is the hardest time, keeping watch through the night vigil and daytime too for difficult births, marauding predators, harrying dogs, even crows waiting to peck out eyes. The shepherd stands ready to correct a breach birth with a long pull, or to skin a dead lamb to help with the adoption of a triplet. What an amazing picture of God right with us in the mess and muddle of life and death, working tirelessly to bring us through all the dangers to the possibility of new life.

Hymn/Song – *suggestions*

How lovely on the mountains, Leonard E. Smith

Shepherd me, O God, Marty Haugen

Bible Reading – *John 10.11–16*

I am the good shepherd. The good shepherd lays down his life for the sheep. The hired hand, who is not the shepherd and does not own the sheep, sees the wolf coming and leaves the sheep and runs away – and the wolf snatches them and scatters them. The hired hand runs away because a hired hand does not care for the sheep. I am the good shepherd. I know my own and my own know me, just as the Father knows me and I know the Father. And I lay down my life for the sheep. I have other sheep that do not belong to this fold. I must bring them also, and they will listen to my voice. So there will be one flock, one shepherd.

Living Word of God,
live in our lives today.

Reflection

It is not surprising that Jesus used so many images and stories from the agricultural world, and particularly shepherding, as most of his hearers would know this world for themselves. The good shepherd, the gate of the sheepfold, the lost sheep, the sheep and the goats, all connected with the life people knew and the God they wanted to know. This is not just a God who waits patiently, who stands ready to help in times of trouble, who guides and protects. This is God in Jesus who lays down his life for the sheep.

Jesus speaks about knowing and being known. With enough stability in farming practices, upland sheep are said to become 'hefted' to their territory; they know its boundaries, where to find water, to avoid dangers and to find shelter. This knowledge and sense of belonging is passed on to each generation.

Silence *(two minutes)*

In the silence we hold these questions:

Do you feel you belong, knowing and being known?
Who would you be willing to lay down your life for?

Conversation *(three minutes)*

We turn to a neighbour and share our responses.

Prayers of Recognition

We bring to God our own vulnerability.
Like new-born lambs we sometimes find ourselves helpless.
Hold us through our first unsteady steps.
(Silence)

I know my own,
and my own know me.

We bring to God our own sense of belonging.
Like hefted sheep, we long to know our boundaries.
Guide and protect us as we learn.
(Silence)

I know my own,
and my own know me.

We bring to God the times when we feel lost or abandoned.
Like the lost sheep, we hope for your reassuring touch.
Find us and lead us home.
(Silence)

I know my own,
and my own know me.

Hymn/Song – *suggestion*

Loving Shepherd of thy sheep, Jane Elizabeth Leeson

Action

We make a simple cross from lengths of wool, to remember the good shepherd who lays down his life for the sheep.

Music – *suggestion*

Chasing sheep is best left to shepherds, Michael Nyman

Hymn/Song – *suggestions*

Faithful Shepherd, feed me, Thomas Benson Pollock

Father hear the prayer we offer, Love Maria Willis

Prayers of Intercession

God the good shepherd, we pray for all shepherds, farmers and vets,
all who are involved in lambing and the care of the flock.
Give them stamina in the long night watches,
vigilance to defend against dangers and predators,
and give them compassion as they care for their sheep.
(Silence)

Faithful shepherd,
feed us.

God the good shepherd, who searches to find the lost,
be with all those who support and care for the vulnerable,
for carers, social workers, probation officers,
all who work at the margins of society.
(Silence)

Faithful shepherd,
feed us.

God the good shepherd, you know your sheep.
May we learn to know your voice and to follow you,
to be guided by you, through all the dangers of this life.
(Silence)

Faithful shepherd,
feed us.

God the gate of the sheepfold, you shelter the sick and suffering ones.
Protect all who struggle today with illness or disability,
all who are living with mental illness or dementia,
and all who care for them.
(Silence)

Faithful shepherd,
feed us.

Lamb of God, you lay down your life for the world.
We remember all who have died recently,
and all who mourn their loss.
Help us to know there is one shepherd, one flock,
together in your care.
(Silence)

Faithful shepherd,
feed us.

Hymn/Song – *suggestions*

Dear Lord and Father of Mankind, John Greenleaf Whittier

Guide me, O thou great Redeemer, William Williams

Blessing

Gate of the sheepfold,
guard us.
Good shepherd,
guide us.
Lamb of God,
lead us home.
May the blessing of God,
Father, Son and Holy Spirit,
be with us always.
Amen.

MAY

All Shall Be Well

Julian of Norwich – Cherished and held in the hand of God

Preparation and Invitation

This service, celebrating the contemplative Julian of Norwich, has a reflective feel and will hold a time of real silence at its heart. You might like to reach out to groups in your community that are interested in reflection, meditation or other mindful practices.

You will need some hazelnuts, enough for everyone to hold one during the prayers. If you can, source them in their shells in the hedgerows, but if this is difficult, use the hazelnut kernels you can buy.

Gathering Music – *suggestion*

Prelude and fugue in F major, BWV 556, Johann Sebastian Bach

Welcome and Introduction

We come to celebrate the unique life of a woman whose name we do not even know! We know of her from her writings, *Revelations of Divine Love*, which is the earliest surviving book by a woman in the English language. We call her Julian of Norwich, named after the church where she lived as an anchorite, a solitary woman of prayer. Today we are invited on a journey of discovery into the heart of God's love for us.

Hymn/Song – *suggestions*

O God, you search me and you know me, Bernadette Farrell

She sits like a bird, John L. Bell and Graham Maule

Opening Psalm

Where can I go from your spirit?
Or where can I flee from your presence?
If I ascend to heaven, you are there;
if I make my bed in Sheol, you are there.
If I take the wings of the morning
and settle at the farthest limits of the sea,
even there your hand shall lead me,
and your right hand shall hold me fast.
If I say, 'Surely the darkness shall cover me,
and the light around me become night',
even the darkness is not dark to you;
the night is as bright as the day,
for darkness is as light to you.

Glory to the Father and to the Son and to the Holy Spirit;
as it was in the beginning, is now and shall be for ever. Amen.
Psalm 139.7–12

Reading – Revelations of Divine Love, *Julian of Norwich, chapter V, Westminster MS*

And in this he showed me a little thing, the quantity of a hazelnut, lying in the palm of my hand, it seemed, and it was as round as any ball. I looked thereupon with the eye of my understanding, and I thought, 'What may this be?' And it was answered generally thus: 'It is all that is made.' I wondered how it could last, for I thought it might suddenly fall to nothing for little cause. And I was answered in my understanding: 'It lasts and ever shall, for God loves it; and so everything has its beginning by the love of God.' In this little thing I saw three properties; the first is that God made it; the second is that God loves it; and the third is that God keeps it.

Reflection

Julian of Norwich lived in a time of plague, the Black Death. When she was 30, in 1373, she became very ill and near to death. She had a series of visions, or 'Showings' as she called them. She recovered from her illness and lived for a further 33 years, using this time to reflect on her experience. Today we know what it is to live in a time of contagion, with Covid-19 affecting the whole world. Her vision of the hazelnut in God's hand is simple but very profound. From the tiny hazelnut Julian is reminded that God holds the immensity of the universe in his hand, holds it all in being. On a more personal level, our lives are held in God's hand and without God loving us into being nothing would exist. When we feel insignificant or overwhelmed by events, we can rest secure in the knowledge that we are held.

Hymn/Song – *suggestions*

When I feel the touch of your hand, Keri Jones and David Matthews

Have faith in God my heart, Bryn Rees

Bible Reading – *Luke 12.22–31*

He said to his disciples, 'Therefore I tell you, do not worry about your life, what you will eat, or about your body, what you will wear. For life is more than food, and the body more than clothing. Consider the ravens: they neither sow nor reap, they have neither storehouse nor barn, and yet God feeds them. Of how much more value are you than the birds! And can any of you by worrying add a single hour to your span of life? If then you are not able to do so small a thing as that, why do you worry about the rest? Consider the lilies, how they grow: they neither toil nor spin; yet I tell you, even Solomon in all his glory was not clothed like one of these. But if God so clothes the grass of the field, which is alive today and tomorrow is thrown into the oven, how much more will he clothe you – you of little faith! And do not keep striving for what you are to eat and what you are to drink, and do not keep worrying. For it is the nations of the world that strive after all these things, and your Father knows that you need them. Instead, strive for his kingdom, and these things will be given to you as well.'

Living Word of God,
live in our lives today.

Reflection

Dealing with our worries is the work of a lifetime. At each new stage there are fresh anxieties to wrestle with! For some it will be the most basic needs for survival, clean water, enough food for today, shelter to sleep. So many who are homeless, or who live below the poverty line, struggle with these each day. In our affluent society, we have other worries around food and clothing. So many people struggle with obesity or eating disorders, or with social media induced anxiety about clothes, image and fashion. Jesus reminds us that our true value comes from within, from knowing we are loved, loved by God. He points us to the natural world: the lilies, the birds of the air, who are clothed more richly than even the wealthiest king. To become immersed in the beauty of the natural world is one of the best antidotes to anxiety. Ann Morisy in her book *Journeying Out* writes about the principle of 'obliquity', where we often find our fulfilment by taking an oblique angle! Studying the wild flowers, watching the birds, can completely absorb us, and we can receive a blessing, a 'cascade of grace', as our worries are reduced to their true proportions.

Julian of Norwich was a contemplative who found peace through silence. In this time of silence we identify the worries that are pre-occupying us today and listen for God's inner prompting of our hearts.

Silence *(five minutes)*

In the silence we hold these questions:

What are you worried about today? Can you lay these worries down? In the stillness, can you sense God prompting you to find him in a new direction?

Music for reflection – *suggestion*

Prelude and fugue in F major, BWV 556, Johann Sebastian Bach

Prayers of Recognition

God's answer to Julian of Norwich in her anxiety was a simple affirmation: 'All shall be well, and all shall be well, and all manner of things shall be well.'

We bring to God all the worries of our lives,
all that preoccupies our minds, growing out of proportion,
waking us in the early hours.
(Silence)

All shall be well, and all shall be well,
and all manner of things shall be well.

We bring to God our fears and phobias,
all that threatens to diminish our lives,
all that curtails our freedom.
(Silence)

All shall be well, and all shall be well,
and all manner of things shall be well.

We bring to God the external pressures that influence us,
the advertisements that entice us,
the standard of living that demands so much from us.
(Silence)

All shall be well, and all shall be well,
and all manner of things shall be well.

We offer to God our openness to the gifts of the natural world,
the lilies of the field, the birds of the air,
the beauty of the earth, the changing of the seasons.
(Silence)

All shall be well, and all shall be well,
and all manner of things shall be well.

Hymn/Song – *suggestions*

Put peace into each other's hands, Fred Kaan

O Lord, hear my prayer, Taizé Community

Prayers of Intercession

As we each take a hazelnut in our hand, we picture God holding us as we pray.

God of compassion, you hold us in your hand, like a hazelnut.
You hold our universe in being.
We thank you for the birds of the air, the flowers of the fields.
Help us to discern our deep connection to your natural world.
(Silence)

Strive for his kingdom,
and these things will be given to you as well.

We pray for all who work to raise awareness of climate change,
the crisis that threatens the natural world, the environment around us
and our own way of life.
Help us to protect nature's diversity and beauty,
by living more sustainably.
(Silence)

Strive for his kingdom,
and these things will be given to you as well.

We pray for our economy, our working lives,
driven by so many demands and pressures to work longer and harder.
We pray for those whose employment is unstable and unpredictable.
We pray for all who struggle to put food on the table and to pay
    the bills.
(Silence)

Strive for his kingdom,
and these things will be given to you as well.

We pray for our families and friends and our local community,
for those who are in unhappy or abusive relationships,
for all who are lonely or isolated.
We pray that we may find ways of including and valuing others.
(Silence)

Strive for his kingdom,
and these things will be given to you as well.

We pray for all who, like Julian of Norwich, struggle with illness,
all who come close to death or mourn the death of loved ones.
We pray for all who are worried about memory loss or
    growing disability.
(Silence)

Strive for his kingdom,
and these things will be given to you as well.

We remember all who have died recently, and those whose memory
    we treasure.
We give thanks for the example and wisdom of Julian of Norwich
and for all that great cloud of witnesses who worship continually
    before your throne.
(Silence)

Strive for his kingdom,
and these things will be given to you as well.

Hymn/Song – *suggestions*

Beauty for brokenness, Graham Kendrick

Like a mighty river flowing, Michael Perry

Blessing

God who holds the hazelnut,
bless us.
God who paints the flower of the field,
bless us.
God who feeds the birds of the air,
bless us.
May the blessing of God,
Father, Son and Holy Spirit,
be with us now and evermore.
Amen.

Daring to Ask

Rogation Sunday – Blessing the growing crops

Preparation and Invitation

If there are any arable or vegetable farmers in your area, or gardeners, allotments or local clubs, it can be good to involve them in this service. Approach them in good time and ask them to prepare some soil, seed and growing crops for display in the service. These can be in containers and can look quite striking. Ideas might be pots of potatoes, wheat, oats, barley, oilseed rape, grass, maize. This can give the local farming and gardening community an opportunity to share what is growing in the area at this time. You will also need a container of soil to be blessed.

Gathering Music – *suggestion*

All things bright and beautiful, John Rutter

Welcome and Introduction

The word Rogation comes from the Latin *rogare*, to ask. Today we come to ask God's blessing on the soil, the seed and the growing crops. We welcome the farming community and all who care for the land. We welcome all gardeners who till the soil and nurture their patch. Today more than ever we have come to realize how some of our practices have denuded the land, and exhausted the soil. We come to ask that God will show us a more sustainable way to live as we honour our planet.

Hymn/Song – *suggestions*

For the beauty of the earth, Folliott Sandford Pierpoint

Dance and sing all the earth, John L. Bell and Graham Maule

Opening Psalm

You visit the earth and water it,
you greatly enrich it;
the river of God is full of water;
you provide the people with grain,
for so you have prepared it.
You water its furrows abundantly,
settling its ridges,
softening it with showers,
and blessing its growth.
Psalm 65.9–10

Reflection

From ancient times we have recognized how important the soil of the earth is for the growing of crops to feed and clothe us. We are bound to the earth and we depend upon it. In Latin *homo* means human, and *humus* means soil; both are derived from the same root word. In Genesis we are reminded, 'you are dust, and to dust you shall return' (Genesis 3.19). In caring for the earth we are caring for ourselves and our children and grandchildren.

We have become disconnected from the soil. We find our food in supermarkets, but often know little of what it takes to bring food from field to fork. In asking for a good harvest, we may be required to change our ways if we want the soil to go on giving. God wants us to be good stewards of the earth. So we dare to ask God to bless our soil, seed and growing crops, knowing that God may ask us to be part of the change that will bring that blessing.

Blessing of the Soil

A pot of soil is brought forward by a local farmer or grower, who says:

We bring this soil, to represent all the land of this community.
We honour the soil, its complex web of life, microorganisms, fungi.
We ask God's blessing for fertility, growth and harvest.

The worship leader responds:

Creator God, bless the earth!

You cause the grass to grow for the cattle,
and plants for people to use,
to bring forth food from the earth,
and wine to gladden the human heart,
oil to make the face shine,
and bread to strengthen the human heart.
Thanks be to God.
Psalm 104.14–15

Blessing of the Seed

*A pot of seeds is brought forward by a local farmer or grower
who says:*

We bring these seeds to represent all that is sown on the land of
    this community.
We honour the advances made in this seed, in resistance, growth
    and yield.
We ask God's blessing for germination, growth and harvest.

The worship leader responds:

Creator God, bless the seed!

Faithfulness will spring up from the ground,
and righteousness will look down from the sky.
The Lord will give what is good,
and our land will yield its increase.
Thanks be to God.
Psalm 85.11–12

Blessing of the Growing Crops

*A pot of growing crops is brought forward by a local farmer or
grower, who says:*

We bring these growing crops to represent all that is growing on the
    land of this community.
We honour the balance of nature that makes for a good harvest.
We ask God's blessing for the maturing and ripening of our crops.

The worship leader responds:

Creator God, bless the growing crops!

For the Lord is good;
his steadfast love endures for ever,
and his faithfulness to all generations.
Thanks be to God.
Psalm 100.5

Hymn/Song – *suggestions*

God, whose farm is all creation, John Arlott

Great is thy faithfulness, Thomas Chisholm

Bible Reading – *Matthew 13.1–9*

That same day Jesus went out of the house and sat beside the lake. Such great crowds gathered around him that he got into a boat and sat there, while the whole crowd stood on the beach. And he told them many things in parables, saying: 'Listen! A sower went out to sow. And as he sowed, some seeds fell on the path, and the birds came and ate them up. Other seeds fell on rocky ground, where they did not have much soil, and they sprang up quickly, since they had no depth of soil. But when the sun rose, they were scorched; and since they had no root, they withered away. Other seeds fell among thorns, and the thorns grew up and choked them. Other seeds fell on good soil and brought forth grain, some a hundredfold, some sixty, some thirty. Let anyone with ears listen!'

Living Word of God,
live in our lives today.

Reflection

It can be hard getting your ideas accepted. Jesus wanted people to hear the good news of God's love, but he found that many things could get in the way of his message. He wanted people to live fruitful lives, fruit that would last. For many years the growing evidence about climate change and environmental damage has fallen on deaf ears and hardened hearts. It has been like seed falling on the path, eaten by birds. More recently there has been some acceptance – we do our recycling, take part in stewardship projects – but little willingness to really change. It is like seed falling on the rocky land, with no depth of soil. As the message about environmental damage has grown more insistent, so there have been many competing claims from vested interests determined to defend their own profits – like seed falling among thorns and being choked. But some seed has been falling on to the good soil, and people are changing, protecting the vitality and structure of the soil, creating space for insects and other diverse wildlife to thrive, looking for a more sustainable pattern of agriculture. If we want to be fruitful, thirty, sixty, a hundredfold into the future, then we will need to let this seed of an idea grow in us.

Silence *(two minutes)*

In the silence we hold these questions:

What kind of soil am I when it comes to the environmental crisis? What needs to change in the way I live?

Conversation

We turn to a neighbour to discuss our response to the questions.

Prayers of Recognition

We bring to God the times when we have been hard-hearted, unwilling even to hear the environmental challenge for ourselves. *(Silence)*

Some seed fell on the path.
Lord, have mercy.

We bring to God the times when we have started to make a change but have slipped back to our old ways. *(Silence)*

Some seed fell on stony ground.
Christ, have mercy.

We bring to God the times when we have been unwilling to change, unwilling to face the impact on our own way of life. *(Silence)*

Some seed fell among thorns.
Lord, have mercy.

God the Sower,
may the good news of your love for us
find the good soil of our hearts,
that we may embrace the changes needed
to care for your creation
and for one another.
May our harvest be sustainable,
some a hundredfold, some sixty, some thirty.
Let anyone with ears listen!
Amen.

Hymn/Song – *suggestions*

Touch the earth lightly, Shirley Erena Murray

Praise and thanksgiving, Albert F. Bayly

Prayers of Intercession

We pray for the farming community,
for all who hold stewardship of the land:
may the Lord give what is good,
that our land may yield its increase.

In the stress and pressure of the growing season,
in responding to a changing climate with new challenges:
may the Lord give what is good,
that our land may yield its increase.

In the uncertainty of changing market conditions,
and in the face of demands to reduce costs:
may the Lord give what is good,
that our land may yield its increase.

We pray for farmers across the world,
those who live with depleted soils and damaged environments:
may the Lord give what is good,
that our land may yield its increase.

We pray for ourselves as consumers;
help us to support those who are caring for the soil:
may the Lord give what is good,
that our land may yield its increase.

We pray for all who are struggling
with illness and disability, with loneliness and stress.
We remember all who have died,
and for those who mourn their loss.
For the Lord is good;
his steadfast love endures for ever,
and his faithfulness to all generations.

Hymn/Song – *suggestions*

I, the Lord of sea and sky, Dan Schutte

For the fruits of his creation, Fred Pratt Green

Blessing

God who sows the seeds of change,
give us ears to hear.
God who tills the soil of our hearts,
give us a willingness to change.
God who grows the fruit of your Spirit,
bring us to a good harvest.
May the blessing of God,
Father, Son and Holy Spirit,
be with us all, evermore.
Amen.

JUNE

Day by Day

Richard of Chichester – Knowing, loving, following

Preparation and Invitation

If you have a prayer group in the church you might like to invite them to take a lead in organizing this service. You will need to give everyone at the service a postcard-sized piece of white card and something to write with. You will also need to set up a table with an image of a large question mark at the centre.

Gathering Music – *suggestion*

A Prayer of St Richard of Chichester, Michael Leighton Jones

Welcome and Introduction

Richard of Chichester was born in Burford, Worcestershire in 1197. From a background of tragedy – the early loss of his parents, impoverishment and hard agricultural work – he managed to gain a place at Oxford, first to learn and then to teach, and later still to become Chancellor of the university. He was ordained and eventually became Bishop of Chichester, although his appointment was opposed by the King, Henry III, who had preferred another candidate, and he spent some time in exile in France.

He is best known for his deathbed prayer. Richard's prayer invites us to encounter Jesus with the whole of ourselves: head, heart and

Medieval wall painting of St Richard of Chichester in the nave of Black Bourton church, Oxfordshire

action. To know Jesus with our minds, to use our intellectual gifts to understand more of God through reason, thinking, study and reflection. To love Jesus with our heart, our emotions, to relate to God through our feelings and passions. And finally, to follow Jesus in our living, to put our faith into action, to allow God to make a difference in all we do.

Hymn/Song – *suggestions*

Rejoice in God's saints, Fred Pratt Green

Praise to the holiest in the height, John Henry Newman

Opening Responses

Thanks be to thee, my Lord Jesus Christ,
for all the benefits thou hast given me,
for all the pains and insults thou hast borne for me.
O most merciful redeemer, friend and brother,
may I know thee more clearly,
love thee more dearly,
follow thee more nearly.

Knowing

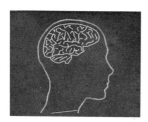

What does it mean to know Jesus? Some early Christian churches thought that there was a secret 'gnosis' or knowledge held by a select few, but Jesus himself worked in the opposite direction. He taught thousands of people that they could know God directly. It is easy to confuse knowing about God with knowing God. There are plenty of courses and books that will impart information about Jesus, about the Bible and the Church, but getting to know God is more personal. It happens when we spend time in the inner conversation of prayer and reflection. God calls us to know him more clearly, to discover the gift of wisdom.

Bible Reading – *Proverbs 2.1–11*

My child, if you accept my words
and treasure up my commandments within you,
making your ear attentive to wisdom
and inclining your heart to understanding;
if you indeed cry out for insight,
and raise your voice for understanding;
if you seek it like silver,
and search for it as for hidden treasures –
then you will understand the fear of the Lord
and find the knowledge of God.
For the Lord gives wisdom;
from his mouth come knowledge and understanding;
he stores up sound wisdom for the upright;
he is a shield to those who walk blamelessly,
guarding the paths of justice
and preserving the way of his faithful ones.
Then you will understand righteousness and justice
and equity, every good path;
for wisdom will come into your heart,
and knowledge will be pleasant to your soul;
prudence will watch over you;
and understanding will guard you.

Living Word of God,
live in our lives today.

Reflection

Knowing God more clearly depends on our commitment to a living
faith that asks questions! It depends on our willingness to invest time
in learning, in reading, discussing, listening and reflecting about our
faith. It also asks for an inner conversation of prayer and silence.

We learn to know more when we use our God-given gifts of intelli-
gence and powers of reasoning. We give thanks for the human mind,
our ability to understand the complexities of the physical world.
We give thanks for the insights of science, which have allowed us to
discover how things have come to be. But many have rejected faith
as being irrational, primitive, not compatible with a scientific world
view. How can we hold together the knowledge of science and the
knowledge of faith? How can we allow these two different kinds of
knowledge to inform and complete each other?

Prayers of Regret

We bring to God our capacity for knowledge and understanding,
knowing that we have often used it to go our own way,
to bring destruction, create weapons, to hurt one another
and to damage our natural world.
(Silence)

O most merciful redeemer, friend and brother,
may we know thee more clearly.

We bring to God the world of science and discovery,
and the arrogance that this kind of knowing can sometimes bring.
We pray for the wisdom to know our own limitations.
(Silence)

O most merciful redeemer, friend and brother,
may we know thee more clearly.

We bring to God our 'head-level' knowledge, our rationality,
knowing that this is only one part of what it is to know.
We ask for grace to respect people who know in different ways.
(Silence)

O most merciful redeemer, friend and brother,
may we know thee more clearly.

God of all knowing,
grant to us true wisdom and understanding,
humility to accept our own limitations,
and a hunger to grow in our knowledge of you.
Amen.

Action

We take a moment to write down the questions that challenge our
faith, and we bring them forward to place around a large question
mark. These may then be used to inform future services, in groups or
in a church magazine.

Hymn/Song – *suggestions*

May the mind of Christ, my Saviour, Kate Barclay Wilkinson

God is our strength from days of old, Michael Forster

Loving

 What does it mean to love Jesus? We move from the arena of head-level knowledge to engage our hearts – the core of our being, our emotions and feelings, our passions. Rationality alone is just one dimension of what it is to be human. Jesus taught us that love is the highest commandment: loving God and loving our neighbour.

Bible Reading – *Matthew 22.34–40*

When the Pharisees heard that he had silenced the Sadducees, they gathered together, and one of them, a lawyer, asked him a question to test him. 'Teacher, which commandment in the law is the greatest?' He said to him, '"You shall love the Lord your God with all your heart, and with all your soul, and with all your mind." This is the greatest and first commandment. And a second is like it: "You shall love your neighbour as yourself." On these two commandments hang all the law and the prophets.'

Living Word of God,
live in our lives today.

Reflection

Love is the most valued quality in human experience. We believe that our capacity to love reflects God's nature in us. Great teachers of prayer have spoken of 'descending with the mind into the heart'. Isaac the Syrian, a seventh-century Christian, wrote, 'Enter the treasure chamber that is within you and then you will discover the treasure chamber of heaven.' In 1 John 4.8 the writer suggests that we can only know God when we love, for 'God is love'. Richard of Chichester's prayer asks that we might love Jesus more dearly. In this time of silence, we make that our prayer too.

Silence *(two minutes)*

In the silence we hold these questions:

How much of my faith stops at head-level knowledge, and how does my faith open me to a deeper heart-level response?
Have I thought through my faith or just accepted it?
What do I feel about God?

Music for Reflection – *suggestion*

A prayer of St Richard of Chichester, Michael Leighton Jones

Conversation

We turn to a neighbour and share some of our reflections.

Hymn/Song – *suggestions*

Purify my heart, Brian Doerksen

Give thanks with a grateful heart, Henry Smith

Following

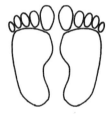 'O let me see thy footmarks and in them plant mine own' – words from the hymn 'O Jesus, I have promised'. Thoughts and feelings are both important, but Richard of Chichester's prayer reminds us that faith must also be embodied. It has to be lived out and to make a difference to the way we live. Jesus called many people to follow him, to live with him on the road, to live like him, to share in his radical acceptance of others, his simplicity and faith. Sharing a meal with Matthew the tax-collector was a way of embodying the good news, that God loves and includes everyone in the kingdom of heaven.

Bible Reading – *Matthew 9.9–13*

As Jesus was walking along, he saw a man called Matthew sitting at the tax booth; and he said to him, 'Follow me.' And he got up and followed him.

And as he sat at dinner in the house, many tax-collectors and sinners came and were sitting with him and his disciples. When the Pharisees saw this, they said to his disciples, 'Why does your teacher eat with tax-collectors and sinners?' But when he heard this, he said, 'Those who are well have no need of a physician, but those who are sick. Go and learn what this means, "I desire mercy, not sacrifice." For I have come to call not the righteous but sinners.'

Living Word of God,
live in our lives today.

Reflection

The Gospel accounts of the calling of Matthew vary slightly in how the event is recorded. Mark and Luke describe Jesus seeing a 'tax-collector called Levi', but Matthew himself makes a subtle difference: 'he saw a man called Matthew sitting at the tax booth'. A man, not a tax-collector! Jesus saw through the labels and externals to the person, the man beneath. Another encounter, with Zacchaeus, a similar act of radical inclusion in a shared supper, led to the tax-collector giving away his fortune and making amends for any he had cheated. Jesus calls us to follow him in learning to see with new eyes, having our attitudes transformed, putting our faith into practice. To follow Jesus more nearly is the work of a lifetime, day by day, one step at a time.

In our prayers of intercession we remember the life of Richard of Chichester and hold in the stream of God's grace all who today are labelled, judged, overlooked or excluded.

Prayers of Intercession

We remember the poverty of Richard's early life after the death of
    his parents.
Compassionate God,
be with all who struggle to make ends meet,
all in low-paid jobs or relying on state support,
all children in care and those who have lost parents.
(Silence)

Redeemer, friend, brother,
day by day, Lord, we pray.

We remember Richard's love of study and valuing of education.
God of wisdom,
be with all who find education difficult,
all who struggle to complete their education because of lack of finance,
all with special educational needs.
May we all know you more clearly.
(Silence)

Redeemer, friend, brother,
day by day, Lord, we pray.

We remember Richard's times of conflict with King Henry III, his
    exile and rejection.
Friend of the friendless,
be with all who today are in exile,
those fleeing war, oppression or poverty,
all needing welcome, shelter and acceptance.
(Silence)

Redeemer, friend, brother,
day by day, Lord, we pray.

We remember Richard's call to love more dearly.
Gracious God,
be with all who struggle to know love,
all who have been disillusioned or let down by others,
all who have been abused,
all who are afraid to trust again.
(Silence)

Redeemer, friend, brother,
day by day, Lord, we pray.

We remember Richard's prayer on his deathbed.
O most merciful redeemer, friend and brother,
hold in your arms of love all who struggle with illness or pain.
Bring healing of body, mind and spirit.
Hold in your arms of love all who have died.
(Silence)

Redeemer, friend, brother,
day by day, Lord, we pray.

Hymn/Song – *suggestions*

Show me how to stand for justice, Martin E. Leckebusch

Fill thou my life, O Lord my God, Horatius Bonar

Blessing

God who reaches out that we might know you,
give us minds to seek you.
Jesus who shows us how to love all, even the unlovely,
give us hearts to love like you.
Spirit who calls us to follow in the ways of peace,
give us the will, day by day, to be changed.
Bless us now, Father, Son and Holy Spirit.
Amen.

Hedgerow Abundance

Midsummer Solstice – Jam jar flower festival

Preparation and Invitation

Flower festivals can be intimidating and expensive events to put on, but a festival using jam-jar displays can allow all ages and levels of expertise to participate, at virtually no cost. You could invite a local school to be involved; it could be woven into their curriculum to produce a jam-jar arrangement of hedgerow or garden flowers, and to bring these to church on the day to offer as their contribution. All sorts of community and gardening groups could be invited to take part in the same way. It would be good to remind people that no special or rare flowers are needed; just choose common ones!

You will need to plan where the jam jars can be placed in church for maximum effect. We have found that they work well down the sides of the aisles and on windowsills.

Gathering Music – *suggestion*

In an English country garden, arr. Percy Grainger

Welcome and Introduction

The midsummer solstice marks the longest day of the year. It has been celebrated by human beings since the dawn of time as a turning point in the year. This 'jam-jar flower festival' gives thanks for the beauty of the earth. It is an expression of creativity, of giving time to look and to see flowers often dismissed as weeds. It points us to Jesus, who urged us not to worry but to consider the lily clothed more richly even than Solomon in all his glory. On the longest day we take a longer look at the world around us.

Hymn/Song – *suggestions*

For the beauty of the earth, Folliott Sandford Pierpoint

Oh, the life of the world, Kathy Galloway

Opening Responses

My beloved speaks and says to me:
'Arise, my love, my fair one,
and come away;
for now the winter is past,
the rain is over and gone.
The flowers appear on the earth;
the time of singing has come,
and the voice of the turtle-dove is heard in our land.
The fig tree puts forth its figs,
and the vines are in blossom;
they give forth fragrance.
Arise, my love, my fair one, and come away.'

Glory to the Father and to the Son and to the Holy Spirit;
as it was in the beginning, is now and shall be for ever. Amen.
Song of Solomon 2.10–13

Reading – Story of a Soul, *St Thérèse of Lisieux*

Jesus deigned to teach me this mystery. He set before me the book of nature; I understood how all the flowers he has created are beautiful, how the splendour of the rose and the whiteness of the lily do not take away the perfume of the little violet or the delightful simplicity of the daisy. I understood that if all the flowers wanted to be roses, nature would lose her springtime beauty, and the fields would no longer be decked out with little wild flowers.

Reflective Walk

As music is played, you are invited to walk around the church, to look more closely at the flower arrangements, to notice the 'delightful simplicity' of the hedgerow and garden flowers.

Music – *suggestion*

D'un vieux jardin, Lili Boulanger

Hymn/Song – *suggestions*

Morning has broken, Eleanor Farjeon

Daisies are our silver, Jan Struther

Bible Reading – *Matthew 6.25–33*

Therefore I tell you, do not worry about your life, what you will eat or what you will drink, or about your body, what you will wear. Is not life more than food, and the body more than clothing? Look at the birds of the air; they neither sow nor reap nor gather into barns, and yet your heavenly Father feeds them. Are you not of more value than they? And can any of you by worrying add a single hour to your span of life? And why do you worry about clothing? Consider the lilies of the field, how they grow; they neither toil nor spin, yet I tell you, even Solomon in all his glory was not clothed like one of these. But if God so clothes the grass of the field, which is alive today and tomorrow is thrown into the oven, will he not much more clothe you – you of little faith? Therefore do not worry, saying, 'What will we eat?' or 'What will we drink?' or 'What will we wear?' For it is the Gentiles who strive for all these things; and indeed your heavenly Father knows that you need all these things. But strive first for the kingdom of God and his righteousness, and all these things will be given to you as well.

Living Word of God,
live in our lives today.

Reflection

What are you worrying about? Most of us carry a sack full of worries with us! Family, job, money, home, health; and it was just the same in Jesus' day. It's easy to *say* 'Don't worry' but harder to do! So Jesus gives a practical alternative: 'Consider the lilies of the field'. It's an invitation to step off the treadmill of our busy lives and simply to 'be' in the moment, to see the beauty in the world around us, in detail. Today we might think of it as mindfulness; in earlier times they called it the 'sacrament of the present moment'. In stopping for long enough to see the beauty and extraordinary colour and form of the flowers all around us, we are entering into the gift that God has provided. It has often been called the 'first bible'. God's first act of revelation is creation itself. Midsummer is the gift of time: time to stop, to pause, to let go of our worries and to contemplate the goodness of God in creation. God knows our needs and always provides. All we must do is stop and look. Let's take a moment of quiet now to do that.

Silence *(two minutes)*

In the silence we hold this question:

What are you worried about at the moment? Take time to lay it down and allow God to hold your worry.

Prayers of Recognition

We bring to God our worries and anxieties,
the tensions and stresses of our lives.
(Silence)

The flowers appear on the earth;
the time of singing has come.

We bring to God our busyness,
the frenetic pace of our lives.
(Silence)

The flowers appear on the earth;
the time of singing has come.

We bring to God our responsibilities,
those who rely on us and make demands on us.
(Silence)

The flowers appear on the earth;
the time of singing has come.

We offer to God this present moment,
our availability and openness to the scripture of creation.
(Silence)

The flowers appear on the earth;
the time of singing has come.

We offer to God our attention in the small things,
our ability to notice and celebrate beauty.
(Silence)

The flowers appear on the earth;
the time of singing has come.

We offer to God our own creativity,
our insight and appreciation of the goodness of creation.
(Silence)

The flowers appear on the earth;
the time of singing has come.

Hymn/Song – *suggestions*

> Creation sings!, Martin E. Leckebusch

> Like a mighty river flowing, Michael Perry

Prayers of Intercession

We pray for the wonder and diversity of nature,
especially that which is overlooked or unnoticed:
for places of outstanding natural beauty,
for nature reserves and for all who protect them,
for farmers who respect the field headlands
and preserve wild spaces.
(Silence)

Consider the lilies;
your Father knows your need.

We pray for all those burdened by worry and stress,
at home, at work or in the wider world,
for those struggling to cope with responsibilities,
and especially for carers.
Give us all grace to live in this present moment,
knowing that today's trouble is enough for today.
(Silence)

Consider the lilies;
your Father knows your need.

We pray for all those who help us to stop and see with new eyes:
for artists and poets,
for all who share gifts of creativity,
for our schools, for children and teachers.
May there be wisdom to find space in the curriculum
to nurture and sustain us as whole people.
(Silence)

Consider the lilies;
your Father knows your need.

We pray for those who face health problems,
especially any awaiting tests or treatment;
for doctors and nurses in our surgeries and hospitals,
that they might offer a holistic approach to our well-being.
We pray for all who mourn the loss of a loved one
and for all those we have loved and whose memory we treasure.
(Silence)

Consider the lilies;
your Father knows your need.

But strive first for the kingdom of God and his righteousness,
and all these things will be given to you as well.

Our Father, who art in heaven,
hallowed be thy name;
thy kingdom come;

thy will be done;
on earth as it is in heaven.
Give us this day our daily bread.
And forgive us our trespasses,
as we forgive those who trespass against us.
And lead us not into temptation;
but deliver us from evil.
For thine is the kingdom,
the power and the glory,
for ever and ever.
Amen.

Hymn/Song – *suggestions*

Morning glory, starlit sky, William Hubert Vanstone

Immortal, invisible, God only wise, Walter Chalmers Smith

Blessing

God of dandelion and daisy,
you hide your beauty in plain sight!
Jesus who considers the lily,
you call us to notice and to wonder!
Holy Spirit present in this and every moment,
you awaken us to the gift of today.
Bless us now, Father, Son and Spirit,
as we journey on with you.
Amen.

JULY

Water of Life

St Swithin – The gift of rain in changing times

Preparation and Invitation

If you have a local environmental group you could invite them to be involved in this service. Or approach individuals connected to charities committed to the developing world, such as Water Aid or Village Water.

You will need to prepare a central focus of water. You could set up a garden water-feature, to provide a sense of movement and sound. Or you could use a large bowl of water, or the church font. If using the font, fill it fully with water. You will need enough pebbles for each person to be given one.

Gathering Music – *suggestion*

The River Cam, Eric Whitacre

Welcome and Introduction

The legend of St Swithin's Day dates from the fourteenth century. Swithin was an Anglo-Saxon Bishop of Winchester. He had asked to be buried outside the church, and when he died in 862 he was buried in the churchyard. However, as he became more revered after his death, it was later planned to move his grave inside the church. Legend has it that this event was delayed by terrible rainstorms that lasted for 40 days. To this day people watch for rain on 15 July as an omen of wet weather to come.

Statue of St Swithin in Stavanger Cathedral, Norway

St Swithin's day if thou dost rain
For forty days it will remain.
St Swithin's day if thou be fair
For forty days 'twill rain nae mare.

Today we come to reflect on the essential gift of water, the source of all life, and to give thanks!

Hymn/Song – *suggestions*

As pants the hart for cooling streams, Nahum Tate and Nicolas Brady

Morning has broken, Eleanor Farjeon

Opening Psalm

Sing to the Lord with thanksgiving;
make melody to our God on the lyre.
He covers the heavens with clouds,
prepares rain for the earth,
makes grass grow on the hills.
He gives to the animals their food,
and to the young ravens when they cry.
Praise the Lord.
Psalm 147.7–9

Opening Prayer

Creator God,
you bless us with the gift of water,
of rainfall in the dry places,
bubbling springs of water to drink,
coursing streams to irrigate the land,
rivers, lakes and the mighty oceans sustaining all life.
Help us to notice the delicate balance of nature,
to understand the impact we have on our environment,
and to honour this precious gift
in the way that we care for all creation,
in the name of Jesus who is the living water,
bubbling up in our hearts and lives.
Amen.

Reading – 'Winter Rain', Christina Rossetti

Every valley drinks,
Every dell and hollow:
Where the kind rain sinks and sinks,
Green of Spring will follow.

Yet a lapse of weeks
Buds will burst their edges,
Strip their wool-coats, glue-coats, streaks,
In the woods and hedges;

Weave a bower of love
For birds to meet each other,
Weave a canopy above
Nest and egg and mother.

But for fattening rain
We should have no flowers,
Never a bud or leaf again
But for soaking showers;

Never a mated bird
In the rocking tree-tops,
Never indeed a flock or herd
To graze upon the lea-crops.

Lambs so woolly white,
Sheep the sun-bright leas on,
They could have no grass to bite
But for rain in season.

We should find no moss
In the shadiest places,
Find no waving meadow-grass
Pied with broad-eyed daisies;

But miles of barren sand,
With never a son or daughter,
Not a lily on the land,
Or lily on the water.

Reflection

Scientists tell us that water is made from two molecules of hydrogen and one of oxygen, which together form the vector of life. Without water, no life is possible! Our blue planet turning in space is well provided with this precious life-giving gift. Christina Rossetti praises the 'fattening rain', recognizing in her poem that all depends on water for its growth and life. Human beings are having more and more of an impact on the balance of nature: our climate is changing, we have witnessed more frequent severe weather conditions, droughts and floods in equal measure. We now know that human choices, like the overproduction in our fields, cutting down of trees, draining of wetlands, eradication of species, can combine to create deserts, 'miles of barren sand' where nothing can grow.

The life-giving gift of water is a powerful metaphor for the spiritual life, and the Bible speaks of God coming down like showers of rain or bubbling up in us as living water. The twelfth-century mystic Hildegard of Bingen brought the two themes together when she wrote of the greening energy of God – *viriditas* – and its opposite, a spiritual dryness or aridity. When we are out of step with God spiritually then it is likely that our actions will be misplaced, and our human impact will be damaging.

Hymn/Song – *suggestions*

Like a mighty river flowing, Michael Perry

Oh the life of the world, Kathy Galloway

Bible Reading – *John* 4.7–15

A Samaritan woman came to draw water, and Jesus said to her, 'Give me a drink.' (His disciples had gone to the city to buy food.) The Samaritan woman said to him, 'How is it that you, a Jew, ask a drink of me, a woman of Samaria?' (Jews do not share things in common with Samaritans.) Jesus answered her, 'If you knew the gift of God, and who it is that is saying to you, "Give me a drink", you would have asked him, and he would have given you living water.' The woman said to him, 'Sir, you have no bucket, and the well is deep. Where do you get that living water? Are you greater than our ancestor Jacob, who gave us the well, and with his sons and his flocks drank from it?' Jesus said to her, 'Everyone who drinks of this water will be thirsty again, but those who drink of the water that I will give them will never be thirsty. The water that I will give will become in them a spring of water gushing up to eternal life.' The woman said to him, 'Sir, give me this water, so that I may never be thirsty or have to keep coming here to draw water.'

Living Word of God,
live in our lives today.

Reflection

This encounter breaks all the rules! As a devout Jew, Jesus should keep his distance from the ritually unclean Samaritan. As a rabbi, Jesus should not be mixing with women, especially those with a reputation. Jesus is asking for help, expressing a need: he is thirsty and tired after a long walk in the heat, and asks the woman for a drink. The conversation is sparky and alive with tension and laughter – you can hear sarcasm and teasing. This encounter is life-giving, both for Jesus and for the Samaritan woman.

Can we learn from Jesus and be able to express our need freely, to ask for help? We often find this hard, having been brought up in a culture that values self-sufficiency. Jesus speaks of the 'living water' that he has to offer, water that quenches an inner thirst, our spiritual aridity or dryness. We sometimes choose to try to slake that thirst, to fill the inner emptiness in ways that only make things worse. It later emerges that the woman has had five husbands and is now in an informal relationship. Our deepest thirst cannot be filled from the outside. We need an inner spring that can only come from God.

Silence *(two minutes)*

In the silence we hold these questions:

Where do I thirst? What feels dried up and parched in me?
What have I been using to try to satisfy that thirst?

Music for Reflection – *suggestion*

The River Cam, Eric Whitacre

Prayers of Recognition

We bring to God all that is dried up in us.
We bring our deepest needs and longings,
our need for love and acceptance,
our need for trusted space and mutual relationship.
(Silence)

For waters shall break forth in the wilderness,
and streams in the desert.
Isaiah 35.6b

We bring to God all that feels empty for us.
We bring our sense of disappointment where life has not been fruitful,
our regrets and losses, our unhappiness.
(Silence)

For waters shall break forth in the wilderness,
and streams in the desert.

We bring to God all that we have used to try to fill the void.
We bring the distractions and distortions of our lives,
the fake alternatives that do not satisfy.
(Silence)

For waters shall break forth in the wilderness,
and streams in the desert.

We bring to God all the impacts of our drives and consumption.
We bring the damage we have done to our world,
the changes we have caused in our climate.
(Silence)

For waters shall break forth in the wilderness,
and streams in the desert.

Action

We bring our dryness to God and we pray for the gift of living water welling up in us to eternal life. You are invited to come forward, bringing your pebble and placing it into a bowl of water. Then dip your finger in the water and make the sign of the cross on your forehead.

Music – *suggestion*

The River Cam, Eric Whitacre

Hymn/Song – *suggestions*

I heard the voice of Jesus say, Horatius Bonar

Spirit of God, come dwell within me, Helen Kennedy

Prayers of Intercession

We pray for all who struggle with a sense of spiritual emptiness,
all who live with deep disappointment or unhappiness.
We pray for the work of churches and chaplaincies,
seeking to bring the good news of God's love.
(Silence)

Living Water,
well up in us to bring life.

We pray for all who struggle with addiction,
all who have become dependent on drugs or alcohol,
seeking to fill the void of their unhappiness.
We pray for all medical workers, counsellors and self-help groups,
that they may bring hope and change to those in need.
(Silence)

Living Water,
well up in us to bring life.

We pray for all who are thirsty today,
all who have to walk miles to collect water,
all who lack even simple sanitation.
We pray for the work of development agencies and charities,
all who dig wells and create latrines.
(Silence)

Living Water,
well up in us to bring life.

We pray for all who are living with the impacts of climate change,
for those who are struggling with increases in sea level,
for those whose homes have been flooded by storms,
for all whose crops have been drowned.
We pray for each of us to live more sustainably
and to reduce our impact on our climate.
(Silence)

Living Water,
well up in us to bring life.

We hold in the stream of God's grace all those we carry in our hearts,
everyone we know and love.
We pray for healing and wholeness for them.
We remember those we have loved and whose loss we mourn.
We commend them into God's love and grace.
(Silence)

Living Water,
well up in us to bring life.

We pray the Lord's Prayer:

**Our Father, who art in heaven,
hallowed be thy name;
thy kingdom come;
thy will be done;
on earth as it is in heaven.
Give us this day our daily bread.
And forgive us our trespasses,
as we forgive those who trespass against us.
And lead us not into temptation;
but deliver us from evil.
For thine is the kingdom,
the power and the glory,
for ever and ever.
Amen.**

Hymn/Song – *suggestions*

Guide me, O thou great Redeemer, William Williams

Hail to the Lord's anointed, James Montgomery

Blessing

God of the pouring rain,
refresh and cleanse us,
bring your greening goodness to our living.
God of the rising brook,
flow in and through us,
bring your refreshing presence to our loving.
God of the wellspring,
sustain us in your depths,
bring your transforming purpose to our action.
May the blessing of God,
Father, Son and Holy Spirit,
be with you now and for ever.
Amen.

No Fear!

Scarecrow Sunday – Facing our fears, finding new heart

Preparation and Invitation

We have hosted a Scarecrow Festival in one of our villages for many years. It brings the community together and generates funds for local projects. Throughout the village, individuals and organizations make scarecrows to display at the roadside, and people from other communities come in large numbers to view the displays. As part of such a festival, or as a separate initiative, this service starts from an exploration of what makes us human, what makes us afraid, what makes us real, and how we are all searching for a new heart. You could approach a local drama group or school to see if they would enact a scene from The Wizard of Oz. *You may like to create a scarecrow to display in the church and be a focus for the service.*

Gathering Music – *suggestion*

We're off to see the wizard, E. Y. Harburg and Harold Arlen

Welcome and Introduction

The job of the scarecrow is to stand in our fields and gardens to scare away the birds, to prevent them from stealing the seeds or eating the flowers, to protect our crops. Made from wood and straw, dressed in old clothes, they stand alone to guard the land. The prophet Jeremiah talked about scarecrows when he warned against the idols and images that pretend to be God. 'Their idols are like scarecrows in a cucumber field, and they cannot speak; they have to be carried, for they cannot walk. Do not be afraid of them, for they cannot do evil, nor is it in them to do good' (Jeremiah 10.5).

Today we shall be thinking about the deep questions that the scarecrow raises: What is real? Do we sometimes pretend to be something we are not? And what are we afraid of?

Hymn/Song – *suggestions*

When morning gilds the skies, tr. Edward Caswall

One more step along the world I go, Sydney Carter

Opening Psalm

You who live in the shelter of the Most High,
who abide in the shadow of the Almighty,
will say to the Lord, 'My refuge and my fortress;
my God, in whom I trust.'
For he will deliver you from the snare of the fowler
and from the deadly pestilence;
he will cover you with his pinions,
and under his wings you will find refuge;
his faithfulness is a shield and buckler.
You will not fear the terror of the night,
or the arrow that flies by day,
or the pestilence that stalks in darkness,
or the destruction that wastes at noonday.

Glory to the Father and to the Son and to the Holy Spirit;
as it was in the beginning, is now and shall be for ever. Amen.
Psalm 91.1–6

Dramatic Reading – *How Dorothy saved the scarecrow*

One of the most loved scarecrows is to be found in *The Wonderful Wizard of Oz* by L. Frank Baum. We hear now of when Dorothy first met him on the yellow brick road.

She bade her friends good-bye, and again started along the road of yellow brick. When she had gone several miles she thought she would stop to rest, and so climbed to the top of the fence beside the road and sat down. There was a great cornfield beyond the fence, and not far away she saw a Scarecrow, placed high on a pole to keep the birds from the ripe corn.

Dorothy leaned her chin upon her hand and gazed thoughtfully at the Scarecrow. Its head was a small sack stuffed with straw, with eyes, nose, and mouth painted on it to represent a face. An old, pointed blue hat, that had belonged to some Munchkin, was perched on his head, and the rest of the figure was a blue suit of clothes, worn and faded, which had also been stuffed with straw. On the feet were some old boots with blue tops, such as every man wore in this country, and the figure was raised above the stalks of corn by means of the pole stuck up its back.

While Dorothy was looking earnestly into the queer, painted face of the Scarecrow, she was surprised to see one of the eyes slowly wink at her. She thought she must have been mistaken at first, for none of the scarecrows in Kansas ever wink; but presently the figure nodded its head to her in a friendly way. Then she climbed down from the fence and walked up to it, while Toto ran around the pole and barked.

'Good day,' said the Scarecrow, in a rather husky voice.

'Did you speak?' asked the girl, in wonder.

'Certainly,' answered the Scarecrow. 'How do you do?'

'I'm pretty well, thank you,' replied Dorothy politely. 'How do you do?'

'I'm not feeling well,' said the Scarecrow, with a smile, 'for it is very tedious being perched up here night and day to scare away crows.'

'Can't you get down?' asked Dorothy.

'No, for this pole is stuck up my back. If you will please take away the pole I shall be greatly obliged to you.'

Dorothy reached up both arms and lifted the figure off the pole, for, being stuffed with straw, it was quite light.

'Thank you very much,' said the Scarecrow, when he had been set down on the ground. 'I feel like a new man.'

Dorothy was puzzled at this, for it sounded queer to hear a stuffed man speak, and to see him bow and walk along beside her.

'Who are you?' asked the Scarecrow when he had stretched himself and yawned. 'And where are you going?'

'My name is Dorothy,' said the girl, 'and I am going to the Emerald City, to ask the Great Oz to send me back to Kansas.'

'Where is the Emerald City?' he inquired. 'And who is Oz?'

'Why, don't you know?' she returned, in surprise.

'No, indeed. I don't know anything. You see, I am stuffed, so I have no brains at all,' he answered sadly.

'Oh,' said Dorothy, 'I'm awfully sorry for you.'

'Do you think,' he asked, 'if I go to the Emerald City with you, that Oz would give me some brains?'

'I cannot tell,' she returned, 'but you may come with me, if you like. If Oz will not give you any brains you will be no worse off than you are now.'

'That is true,' said the Scarecrow. 'You see,' he continued confidentially, 'I don't mind my legs and arms and body being stuffed, because I cannot get hurt. If anyone treads on my toes or sticks a pin into me, it doesn't matter, for I can't feel it. But I do not want people to call me a fool, and if my head stays stuffed with straw instead of with brains, as yours is, how am I ever to know anything?'

'I understand how you feel,' said the little girl, who was truly sorry for him. 'If you will come with me I'll ask Oz to do all he can for you.'

'Thank you,' he answered gratefully.

They walked back to the road. Dorothy helped him over the fence, and they started along the path of yellow brick for the Emerald City.

Toto did not like this addition to the party at first. He smelled around the stuffed man as if he suspected there might be a nest of rats in the straw, and he often growled in an unfriendly way at the Scarecrow.

'Don't mind Toto,' said Dorothy to her new friend. 'He never bites.'

'Oh, I'm not afraid,' replied the Scarecrow. 'He can't hurt the straw. Do let me carry that basket for you. I shall not mind it, for I can't get tired. I'll tell you a secret,' he continued, as he walked along. 'There is only one thing in the world I am afraid of.'

'What is that?' asked Dorothy; 'the Munchkin farmer who made you?'

'No,' answered the Scarecrow; 'it's a lighted match.'

Reflection

In *The Wonderful Wizard of Oz*, Dorothy journeyed along the yellow brick road to try to find the Emerald City. On the way she encountered several characters who were also searching for something. The scarecrow thought he had no brains, and hoped to find some, but in fact proved he was intelligent by coming up with all sorts of solutions to the problems they encountered on the way. How often do we under-estimate ourselves, feeling that we lack something? We sometimes try to bolster our confidence by 'power dressing', adopting an image that may be far from what we are feeling inside. Students at college some-times speak of the 'imposter syndrome', where they don't feel capable of working at the level they find themselves. Michael Mayne, a former Dean of Westminster, spoke of how uncomfortable it is when our 'inscape' doesn't match our 'landscape'.

God sees the real heart of who we are, and calls us into a lifelong journey of becoming more and more real, feeling less afraid, 'ringing true', our insides matching our outsides. Like the scarecrow, we are called to journey and to grow.

When Jesus was arrested he faced the scarecrow – the empty pomp and show of the puppet king Herod who could only pretend to be power-ful. Jesus refused to engage with him. The Roman governor Pontius Pilate wielded huge political power but he was afraid of the crowds, and though he wanted to release Jesus he was unable to. Again, his power was not real; he was another scarecrow! Jesus was then mocked, dressed up as a king and hoisted, like a scarecrow, on to a cross for public display. But unlike Herod or Pilate, Jesus was not a scarecrow. His kingship was real, and even death could not contain him.

Hymn/Song – *suggestions*

Though pilgrim strangers here below, Timothy Dudley-Smith

Thank you for the summer morning, Susan Sayers

Bible Reading – *Ezekiel 36.24–28*

I will take you from the nations, and gather you from all the coun-tries, and bring you into your own land. I will sprinkle clean water upon you, and you shall be clean from all your uncleannesses, and from all your idols I will cleanse you. A new heart I will give you, and a new spirit I will put within you; and I will remove from your body the heart of stone and give you a heart of flesh. I will put my spirit within you, and make you follow my statutes and be careful to observe my ordinances. Then you shall live in the land that I gave to your ancestors; and you shall be my people, and I will be your God.

Living Word of God,
live in our lives today.

Reflection

The prophet Ezekiel tells of how God promises to give us a new heart, a new spirit, calling us to become who we are really meant to be. To do this we need to face up to our fears, to find our real confidence in who we are, allowing our outside image to match our inside reality.

Silence *(two minutes)*

In the silence we hold these questions:

What am I afraid of?
How real am I? Does my inscape match my landscape?
What makes me feel inadequate?

Music for reflection – *suggestion*

Goldberg Variations, BWV 988 – Aria, Johann Sebastian Bach

Prayers of Recognition

We bring to God all that makes us fearful.
As we hold it in our prayer,
we ask for discernment and wisdom
to see through the trappings of the scarecrows of our lives,
to recognize what is real and what is false.
(Silence)

You will not fear the terror of the night,
or the arrow that flies by day.

We bring to God the times when we feel inadequate,
when we doubt ourselves,
when we feel we must pretend.
(Silence)

You will not fear the terror of the night,
or the arrow that flies by day.

We bring to God who we are on the inside
and who we try to be on the outside.
(Silence)

You will not fear the terror of the night,
or the arrow that flies by day.

We open ourselves to God's life-long journey of discovery
to become who God truly intends us to be.
(Silence)

My refuge and my fortress,
my God, in whom I trust.

We open our whole selves to God,
our inner self, our outer image,
to become whole people who ring true.
(Silence)

My refuge and my fortress,
my God, in whom I trust.

We give thanks for our hidden strengths and gifts,
and we offer them to God.
(Silence)

My refuge and my fortress,
my God, in whom I trust.

Hymn/Song – *suggestions*

Seek ye first the kingdom of God, Karen Lafferty

O, the love of my Lord is the essence, Estelle White

Prayers of Intercession

We pray for all in positions of power and responsibility,
for public figures, politicians, leaders of the nations,
for all who must live in the glare of publicity, developing a
 public persona,
all who have to live with criticism and hostility.
(Silence)

A new heart I will give you,
and a new spirit I will put within you.

We pray for all who hold demanding roles in life
yet who live with a sense of inadequacy, undervaluing themselves;
for those who have struggled to be recognized because of
   their background,
for those who live with self-doubt.
(Silence)

A new heart I will give you,
and a new spirit I will put within you.

We pray for all those who are afraid to look inside,
all who avoid times of reflection or self-examination
for fear of lifting the lid on a can of worms,
for fear of discovering emptiness or inadequacy.
(Silence)

A new heart I will give you,
and a new spirit I will put within you.

We pray for those who are vulnerable and easily overwhelmed;
those who are so open-hearted that they take on the worries of
   the world,
those who struggle with stress and poor mental health.
(Silence)

A new heart I will give you,
and a new spirit I will put within you.

As Jesus taught us we pray:

Our Father, who art in heaven,
hallowed be thy name;
thy kingdom come;
thy will be done;
on earth as it is in heaven.
Give us this day our daily bread.
And forgive us our trespasses,
as we forgive those who trespass against us.
And lead us not into temptation;
but deliver us from evil.
For thine is the kingdom,
the power and the glory,

for ever and ever.
Amen.

Hymn/Song – *suggestions*

There in God's garden, Erik Routley

O Lord my God, Stuart K. Hine

Blessing

God who has promised to give us new heart, new spirit,
bless us now with a sense of inner confidence,
to live lives that ring true, inside and out!
Jesus who was dressed up like a scarecrow,
hoisted on a cross and made a mockery of,
bless us now with your courage to remain true,
to face down all that is empty and false.
Spirit who leads us into all truth,
bless us now with energy for the journey,
as we follow the yellow brick road of our becoming.
Amen.

AUGUST

First Fruits

Lammastide – Offering the best of ourselves

Preparation and Invitation

Lammas Day, celebrated on 1 August, is one of the traditional agricultural festivals. You may like to invite local farmers and farmworkers to attend. The barley harvest may well be in by the beginning of August, so if it is grown locally you could ask a farmer to supply some grain to have in church and to offer in the service.

Some of the grain could be ground to produce flour, which can be made into a barley loaf to be shared in the service. Or a local baker could be asked to make a loaf for you from flour made from the harvested grain.

You will also need to ask another person to offer a symbol of their working or productive life in the service.

A child or young person needs to be asked to offer a picture they have created for the service. This could be a Sunday school activity or something prepared by a family in advance.

The church can be decorated with barley sheaves. If you can cut some green earlier in the season and hang it upside down to dry, this will produce an attractive sheaf.

You will need some bread to share later in the service, and this can be placed as a central focus

Gathering Music – *suggestion*

John Barleycorn, Martin Carthy

Welcome and Introduction

Lammas, or 'loaf-mass', is one of the oldest of the traditional agricultural festivals, celebrating the first grain harvest of the season. Its roots stretch back to Old Testament times and to the offering of the first fruit of the barley harvest by the people of Israel. People working the land would have been eking out their stores of grain, eagerly waiting for the new harvest and a relief to hunger. Today when we have so much food flown or shipped to us from around the world, it is easy to lose touch with the rhythm of the seasons and the feeling of anticipation at the coming of the harvest. In this service we will reflect on what are the first fruits of our lives, and we will offer them to God.

Hymn/Song – *suggestions*

To thee, O Lord, our hearts we raise, W. Chatterton Dix

Fair waved the golden corn, John Hampden Gurney

Opening Prayer

God of the growing grain,
of the abundant earth,
of the harvest of our hands,
you have blessed us with fruitful lands,
providing more than enough for our needs,
with plenty to share.
Give us thankful hearts in this time of gathering.
Grant us a generosity of spirit,
to provide for those who go hungry.
May we offer you the first fruits of our lives,
the very best that we have,
that we in turn may become a blessing,
as we follow in the footsteps of your Son,
Jesus, Lord of the Harvest.
Amen.

Opening Psalm

When the Lord restored the fortunes of Zion,
we were like those who dream.
Then our mouth was filled with laughter,
and our tongue with shouts of joy;
then it was said among the nations,
'The Lord has done great things for them.'
The Lord has done great things for us,
and we rejoiced.
Restore our fortunes, O Lord,
like the watercourses in the Negeb.
May those who sow in tears
reap with shouts of joy.
Those who go out weeping,
bearing the seed for sowing,
shall come home with shouts of joy,
carrying their sheaves.

Glory to the Father and to the Son and to the Holy Spirit;
as it was in the beginning, is now and shall be for ever. Amen.
Psalm 126

Bible Reading – *Leviticus 23.9–14*

The Lord spoke to Moses: Speak to the people of Israel and say to them: When you enter the land that I am giving you and you reap its harvest, you shall bring the sheaf of the first fruits of your harvest to the priest. He shall raise the sheaf before the Lord, that you may find acceptance; on the day after the sabbath the priest shall raise it. On the day when you raise the sheaf, you shall offer a lamb a year old, without blemish, as a burnt-offering to the Lord. And the grain-offering with it shall be two-tenths of an ephah of choice flour mixed with oil, an offering by fire of pleasing odour to the Lord; and the drink-offering with it shall be of wine, one-fourth of a hin. You shall eat no bread or parched grain or fresh ears until that very day, until you have brought the offering of your God: it is a statute for ever throughout your generations in all your settlements.

Living Word of God,
live in our lives today.

Reflection

It is so easy to take things for granted – the abundance of food from around the world available to us at the click of a computer mouse, and in every corner shop and supermarket. The pandemic has reminded us of scarcity, with empty shelves and anxious hoarding. We so easily forget the giver of all life, God who gives life and growth. Many of the statutes in Leviticus are given to maintain this connection. We should bring the first fruits of our harvest – and not just the first but the very best of what we have, without blemish. The offering of our fruitfulness is to be the first fruits, not the fag-ends, of our lives! We offer to God the best of ourselves, not just the loose change we happen to have left over.

Silence *(two minutes)*

In the silence we hold these questions:

What are your first fruits? What is fruitful in your life at this moment? Could you offer your gifts, your abilities, to God? How? Is it time to review your financial giving?

Prayers of Recognition

We take time to notice what we have been taking for granted:
the material well-being of our lives,
the availability of food and products from around the world.
(Silence)

Lord, have mercy.
Lord, have mercy.

We take time to notice who we have been taking for granted:
the unseen chain of farmers, processors, transporters and shopkeepers,
the forgotten faces of cleaners, waste collectors, low-paid workers.
(Silence)

Christ, have mercy.
Christ, have mercy.

We take time to notice the presence of God, often taken for granted:
the many blessings in our lives, the gift of life itself,

the grace and mercy that meets us when we fall.
(Silence)

Lord, have mercy.
Lord, have mercy.

Assurance of Forgiveness

Ever-giving God,
your love pours forth like light from the sun,
whether accepted, rejected or ignored.
As we turn towards your light,
as we remember your abundant provision,
as we seek to amend our lives,
we hear your word of grace:
'Your sins are forgiven ... Your faith has saved you; go in peace'
(Luke 7.48–50).
Thanks be to God.
Amen.

Hymn/Song – *suggestions*

In the fullness of the summer time (A Lammastide carol),
Stephen Southgate

Bring to God the first fruits, Tony Ingleby

Bible Reading – *1 Corinthians 15.12–22*

Now if Christ is proclaimed as raised from the dead, how can some
of you say there is no resurrection of the dead? If there is no resurrection of the dead, then Christ has not been raised; and if Christ has
not been raised, then our proclamation has been in vain and your
faith has been in vain. We are even found to be misrepresenting God,
because we testified of God that he raised Christ – whom he did not
raise if it is true that the dead are not raised. For if the dead are not
raised, then Christ has not been raised. If Christ has not been raised,
your faith is futile and you are still in your sins. Then those also who
have died in Christ have perished. If for this life only we have hoped
in Christ, we are of all people most to be pitied.

But in fact Christ has been raised from the dead, the first fruits of
those who have died. For since death came through a human being,

the resurrection of the dead has also come through a human being; for as all die in Adam, so all will be made alive in Christ.

Living Word of God,
live in our lives today.

Reflection

Have you ever caught yourself trying to bargain with God? 'If you will do this, I promise to be good!' There is an echo of this 'transactional' approach in all the sacrifices set out in the Old Testament. The people tried to appease an angry God with their offerings, they tried to wipe away their sins by paying for them. There is a strand throughout the Bible of God saying, 'I don't want or need your offerings', and Jesus embodied this by taking the place of the sacrifice: 'the Lamb of God who takes away the sin of the world' (John 1.29). In this passage Jesus has become the 'first fruits'; his self-offering has brought a harvest of resurrection life for everyone. Bargaining with God doesn't work! All we can do is to receive the gift of God's grace with thankful hearts.

Silence *(two minutes)*

In the silence we hold these questions:

Have you ever tried to bargain with God? How did it turn out?
What have been the first fruits of your faith? How has it changed you?

Prayers of Intercession

We pray for the farming community as they work to bring in
 the harvest.
We give thanks for all who work on the land.
We pray for all who have struggled with difficult conditions,
in the climate, the market, in their own lives.
(Silence)

Lord of the harvest,
hear us, we pray.

We pray for our productive lives.
As we offer the first fruits of our working,
we give thanks for employment and opportunity to thrive.

We pray for all who are unhappy in their work,
all who are unemployed, all who are undervalued.
(Silence)

Lord of the harvest,
hear us, we pray.

We pray for opportunities to be creative and find rest.
We give thanks for our hobbies and interests.
We pray for all who are overstretched and overburdened,
especially for informal carers, who are unsupported.
(Silence)

Lord of the harvest,
hear us, we pray.

We pray for all who feel useless,
those who are becoming less able,
through chronic illness or dementia, through disability or loss.
We pray that we may find new ways to be creative and to live well.
(Silence)

Lord of the harvest,
hear us, we pray.

We remember all who have died recently
and all whose memory we treasure –
the many ways their lives have touched and enriched our lives.
We give thanks that they now enjoy the first fruit of the resurrection.
(Silence)

Lord of the harvest,
hear us, we pray.

As Jesus taught us, we pray:

Our Father, who art in heaven,
hallowed be thy name;
thy kingdom come;
thy will be done;
on earth as it is in heaven.
Give us this day our daily bread.

And forgive us our trespasses,
as we forgive those who trespass against us.
And lead us not into temptation;
but deliver us from evil.
For thine is the kingdom,
the power and the glory,
for ever and ever.
Amen.

Hymn/Song – *suggestions*

I am the bread of life, Suzanne Toolan

O give thanks (The Lord is marching out), Graham Kendrick

Offering of First Fruits

A farmer brings a container of grain and says:

We bring this grain, the first fruits of our harvest:
the gift of God to us,
the work of our hands, of our minds and of our hearts;
and we offer our first fruits.
Thanks be to God.

A baker brings a Lammas loaf and says:

We bring the Lammas loaf, first fruits of our baking:
the gift of God to us,
the work of our hands, of our minds and of our hearts;
and we offer our first fruits.
Thanks be to God.

Another person brings a symbol of their working life and says:

We bring this symbol, to represent all our productive lives:
the gift of God to us,
the work of our hands, of our minds and of our hearts;
and we offer our first fruits.
Thanks be to God.

A child brings a picture they have created and says:

We bring this picture, to represent all our creativity and play:
the gift of God to us,
the work of our hands, of our minds and of our hearts;
and we offer our first fruits.
Thanks be to God.

The service leader receives the symbolic gifts and says:

Thanks be to God for all the blessings of our fruitfulness!
Give us grace not to take them for granted
but to receive them, and so to offer ourselves,
as living sacrifices, holy and acceptable in your sight;
in Jesus' name we pray.
Amen.

Sharing the Lammas Loaf

The Lammas loaf is broken and given to a child to distribute to everyone present.

We eat and reflect in silence.

Prayer of Thanksgiving

Bread of our living,
first fruits of our working,
abundance of God in creation,
be in our sharing,
our living and offering.
We thank you for all our blessings.
Amen.

Hymn/Song – *suggestions*

Praise and thanksgiving, Albert F. Bayly

To God be the glory, Frances Jane van Alstyne

Blessing

God who gives freely,
bless us, with eyes to notice your gifts.
Jesus who gave everything for us,
bless us, in the first fruits of your resurrection.
Holy Spirit who gives life and every good gift,
bless us, as we offer ourselves now.
May the blessing of God,
Father, Son and Holy Spirit,
be with you now and for ever.
Amen.

Gathering the Fragments

Outdoor Service – Feeding the multitude

Preparation and Invitation

The summer months can sometimes allow us to venture outside for worship! It's easy to get stuck in our buildings with all their history and tradition, and to think that this is the only way to worship. Coming outside can allow for more flexibility and a freedom to do new things. It can also help to reconnect us with the experience of the early disciples. Jesus did most of his ministry outside, in the marketplace, beside the lake or in the wilderness. In a time when far fewer people come to church and the culture of church services can be unfamiliar and off-putting, it can help for us to take church outside the four walls of the building and to recapture some of the simplicity and freedom that comes from being in the open air. In planning a service outside we can take heart from the experience of Forest Schools, who manage to operate outside come rain, come shine! We have held services in fields, parks, farm buildings, under canvas shelters and even under umbrellas. Of course, it might even be fine weather!

Worship in the park, on a farm or even in the churchyard can be advertised widely as something different. It can be combined with family games and a picnic, or with a farm tour or an organized walk. It may be necessary to seek permission of the local authorities or a landowner to hold the outdoor service.

You will need to plan how to provide musical accompaniment, whether live music or recorded, with possibly some form of amplification. Some of the church members could be asked to be active in welcoming people and inviting them to join in. Music can set the scene and draw the attention of passers-by, so choose some that will connect with people.

Gathering Music – *suggestion*

Maddy Prior and the Carnival Band sing a selection of gallery hymns on the album *Sing Lustily and with Good Courage*

Welcome and Introduction

In the earliest days Jesus gathered people together in the open air – not in a church or temple but in the marketplace, beside the lake or in the wilderness. He talked about the things that people knew in their everyday lives, like sheep and goats, fish and bread. He made people laugh. He challenged them to think about God in a new way. 'Let those who have ears – listen!' Today we meet in his name, and in his way, so I say again: 'Let those who have ears – listen!'

Hymn/Song – *suggestions*

Fill your hearts with joy and gladness, Timothy Dudley-Smith

O worship the King, Robert Grant

Opening Psalm

Bless the Lord, O my soul.
O Lord my God, you are very great.
You cause the grass to grow for the cattle,
and plants for people to use,
to bring forth food from the earth,
and wine to gladden the human heart,
oil to make the face shine,
and bread to strengthen the human heart.
The trees of the Lord are watered abundantly,
the cedars of Lebanon that he planted.
In them the birds build their nests;
the stork has its home in the fir trees.

The high mountains are for the wild goats;
the rocks are a refuge for the coneys.
You have made the moon to mark the seasons;
the sun knows its time for setting.
You make darkness, and it is night,
when all the animals of the forest come creeping out.
The young lions roar for their prey,
seeking their food from God.
When the sun rises, they withdraw
and lie down in their dens.
People go out to their work
and to their labour until the evening.

Glory to the Father and to the Son and to the Holy Spirit;
as it was in the beginning, is now and shall be for ever. Amen.
Psalm 104.1, 14–23

Thanksgiving for Creation

We each take a few minutes to look more closely at the world around
us, to move, to notice, to appreciate the beauty of our world.
People may like to gather common wildflowers, like daisies or but-
tercups, or grass stems, stones or leaves, and bring them together on
a central table or rug as a focus for thanksgiving. Once all has been
gathered, a central candle may be lit.

With the psalmist, we give thanks for the diversity of the
    natural world,
for the intricate beauty and complexity found in each flower.
(Silence)

Give glory to God!
Glory to God in the highest!

We give thanks for the evidence of God's goodness written
    into creation.
We wonder at the subtle balance of nature.
(Silence)

Give glory to God!
Glory to God in the highest!

We give thanks for the process of evolution,
for the freedom of all creation to become what it may become.
(Silence)

Give glory to God!
Glory to God in the highest!

We give thanks for the productivity and abundance of creation,
giving us all we need for life – life in all its fullness.
(Silence)

Give glory to God!
Glory to God in the highest!

We pause to notice signs of human activity in the landscape.
We give thanks for human ingenuity and invention,
which has enabled us to harness the power of nature.
(Silence)

Give glory to God!
Glory to God in the highest!

Prayers of Penitence

But we have sometimes trampled creation,
distorting the balance of nature,
damaging the diversity of life on this planet.
(Silence)

Lord, hear our sorrow.
Give us time to change our ways.

We have polluted the air, the land, the sea,
dumping toxic waste in our throwaway culture,
changing our climate with unlooked-for consequences.
(Silence)

Lord, hear our sorrow.
Give us time to change our ways.

We have taken resources without heed of the consequences.
We allow so many to live in poverty
while we have more than we need.
(Silence)

Lord, hear our sorrow.
Give us time and grace to change our ways.

Hymn/Song – *suggestions*

Lord, you created a world rich in splendour, Nick Fawcett

Lord of creation, to you be all praise, Jack C. Winslow

Bible Reading – *Matthew 14.13–21*

Now when Jesus heard this, he withdrew from there in a boat to a deserted place by himself. But when the crowds heard it, they followed him on foot from the towns. When he went ashore, he saw a great crowd; and he had compassion for them and cured their sick. When it was evening, the disciples came to him and said, 'This is a deserted place, and the hour is now late; send the crowds away so that they may go into the villages and buy food for themselves.' Jesus said to them, 'They need not go away; you give them something to eat.' They replied, 'We have nothing here but five loaves and two fish.' And he said, 'Bring them here to me.' Then he ordered the crowds to sit down on the grass. Taking the five loaves and the two fish, he looked up to heaven, and blessed and broke the loaves, and gave them to the disciples, and the disciples gave them to the crowds. And all ate and were filled; and they took up what was left over of the broken pieces, twelve baskets full. And those who ate were about five thousand men, besides women and children.

Living Word of God,
live in our lives today.

Reflection

Jesus loved to come out into the countryside, to find a deserted spot, to have some time to rest and think and to pray. He calls us to come out of the narrow confines of our church buildings, out of the narrow confines of our thinking, to experience the wide open spaces of God's love for us and for the whole world. All this is expressed in a simple meal described in Matthew's Gospel, with broken bread and shared fish, a picnic in the wilderness that shows us the kingdom of heaven! Where we think that there is not enough to go round and resources are scarce, Jesus breaks and shares the bread and everyone is fed. Nothing is wasted: even the leftover fragments are gathered up, twelve baskets full! Let's take a few moments of quiet to think about how God calls us to live in the kingdom where all are fed and nothing is wasted.

Silence *(two minutes)*

In the silence we hold these questions:

Who is left outside? Who goes unfed? What is wasted?
How can that change? How can we change?

Action

We take something from the central display we gathered earlier and give it to someone we do not know very well. Together we share some of our reflections.

Music – *suggestion*

Maddy Prior and the Carnival Band – hymns

Hymn/Song – *suggestions*

There's a wideness in God's mercy, Frederick William Faber

I come with joy, a child of God, Brian Wren

Prayers of Intercession

In the abundance of bread and fishes, enough to feed the multitude, bless all those who go hungry today.
Help us to share what we have.
(Silence)

Open our minds and hearts
to the wideness of your mercy.

In the wideness of welcome, enough to include everyone,
bless all who are lonely or left out today.
Help us to welcome all to your feast.
(Silence)

Open our minds and hearts
to the wideness of your mercy.

In the gathering of fragments, so that nothing is lost,
bless all who feel undervalued, unnoticed, unwanted.
Help us to value all in your name.
(Silence)

Open our minds and hearts
to the wideness of your mercy.

In the love of God expressed in the natural world, in all its beauty
    and balance,
bless all those who work to repair the damage we have done,
as we learn to change our ways.
(Silence)

Open our minds and hearts
to the wideness of your mercy.

Jesus taught his friends to pray for God's kingdom to come, saying:

**Our Father, who art in heaven,
hallowed be thy name;
thy kingdom come;
thy will be done;
on earth as it is in heaven.
Give us this day our daily bread.
And forgive us our trespasses,
as we forgive those who trespass against us.
And lead us not into temptation;
but deliver us from evil.
For thine is the kingdom,
the power and the glory,
for ever and ever.
Amen.**

Hymn/Song – *suggestions*

Father, Lord of all creation, Stewart Cross

For the beauty of the earth, Folliott Sandford Pierpoint

Blessing

God of the wide open skies,
the beauty of the landscape, the mystery of life,
bless us with wonder at your generous provision.
Jesus who fed the multitude,
feeding all in the feast of heaven on earth,
bless us now as we welcome all in your name.
Spirit who draws us into new patterns of belonging and community,
gathering the fragments of our lives, healing our brokenness,
bless us now and gather us into the family of God's people.
Amen.

SEPTEMBER

Horses and Humans

Riders' Service – Celebrating a unique partnership

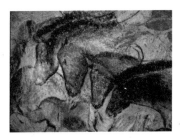

The Dappled Horses of Pech-Merle.
Palaeolithic cave painting

Preparation and Invitation

This is essentially an outdoor service, with people gathered in a semi-circle and horses with riders mounted positioned behind the congregation. You will need to decide the best setting for your service. It has worked very well at a local riding stables that enabled us to use their facilities. It has worked equally well in a field near church. Or you could hold it in a churchyard if there is space. We invite people to come early for a bacon roll and mug of tea, which is always popular!

Riders could be invited to take part in leading sections of the service, in readings or in an interview. There is provision in the service for an interview with a rider about a 'unique partnership'.

It is worth consulting with local stables to check that your planned date doesn't cut across other equine events. There may be a local branch of Riding for the Disabled that might like to be involved. You could invite local vets, blacksmiths or farm suppliers. You will need to publicize the event well in advance, and see if there are any horse-specific social media groups that you could access.

We usually take a mobile keyboard to accompany the singing, and set up a table and candles as a visual focus for the worship. You will need to provide chairs or straw bales for seating.

Welcome and Introduction

From the dawn of time, humans and horses have coexisted in a developing partnership. Cave paintings of horses in France date from 30,000 years ago. The first domestication of horses 6,000 years ago took place on the grasslands of Ukraine. The Uffington Horse from the Bronze Age was worshipped as divine. Horses have added their strength and energy to agriculture, to warfare, to transport, for leisure and recreation, for sport and for therapy. Horses and humans have learned to work together in a rich and complex partnership. Today we come to celebrate this relationship, to give thanks for our horses and to bless them in God's name.

Hymn – *suggestions*

Ride on, ride on in majesty, Henry Hart Milman

Morning has broken, Eleanor Farjeon

Reflection

In the growing partnership between humans and horses we have been able to move away from a purely exploitative relationship to one of companionship and mutual pleasure. Once horses served our needs, pulling the plough, being ridden for transportation or harnessed to carts and carriages. Some worked down in the dark of the mines, some pulled barges along canals. Horses led the charge in battles or carried heavy loads of munitions to the front line.

Many of the references to horses in the Bible are to their use in time of war: they were used by the Egyptians to pursue the fleeing Israelites, and were often held up as an example of human power, rather than a reliance on God's strength. But in these words from the book of Job, the writer captures something of the essence of the horse. God reminds Job of the wonder and complexity of creation.

Opening Responses

Do you give the horse its might?
Do you clothe its neck with mane?
Do you make it leap like the locust?
Its majestic snorting is terrible.
It paws violently, exults mightily;
it goes out to meet the weapons.
It laughs at fear, and is not dismayed;
it does not turn back from the sword.
Upon it rattle the quiver,
the flashing spear, and the javelin.
With fierceness and rage it swallows the ground;
it cannot stand still at the sound of the trumpet.
When the trumpet sounds, it says 'Aha!'
From a distance it smells the battle,
the thunder of the captains, and the shouting.

Glory to the Father and to the Son and to the Holy Spirit;
as it was in the beginning, is now and shall be for ever. Amen.
Job 39.19–25

Interview

A unique partnership – a personal experience of working with horses.

Reading – *St Martin of Tours*

St Martin was born around AD 316, the son of a Roman cavalry officer. At the age of 15 he joined the cavalry himself and he is almost always depicted astride a horse. He found that his Christian faith led him away from the army, and he became a monk and a hermit. In time he became Bishop of Tours. The most famous legend about his life is that when he was riding into Amiens as a soldier he came across a beggar shivering with cold. Moved with compassion, Martin immediately used his sword to cut his own warm cloak into two pieces and gave half to the beggar. Later he had a dream where it was Jesus in place of the beggar, and he realized that in giving to the beggar, he had been giving to Jesus.

157

Hymn – *suggestions*

When a knight won his spurs, Jan Struther

Lord, you call us to a journey, Nick Fawcett

Bible Reading – *Matthew 25.31–40*

When the Son of Man comes in his glory, and all the angels with him, then he will sit on the throne of his glory. All the nations will be gathered before him, and he will separate people one from another as a shepherd separates the sheep from the goats, and he will put the sheep at his right hand and the goats at the left. Then the king will say to those at his right hand, 'Come, you that are blessed by my Father, inherit the kingdom prepared for you from the foundation of the world; for I was hungry and you gave me food, I was thirsty and you gave me something to drink, I was a stranger and you welcomed me, I was naked and you gave me clothing, I was sick and you took care of me, I was in prison and you visited me.' Then the righteous will answer him, 'Lord, when was it that we saw you hungry and gave you food, or thirsty and gave you something to drink? And when was it that we saw you a stranger and welcomed you, or naked and gave you clothing? And when was it that we saw you sick or in prison and visited you?' And the king will answer them, 'Truly I tell you, just as you did it to one of the least of these who are members of my family, you did it to me.'

Living Word of God,
live in our lives today.

Reflection

The parable of the sheep and the goats echoes the legend of St Martin cutting his cloak in half and sharing it with the beggar. The righteous were surprised to be chosen, and asked 'when was it that we saw you' hungry, naked, sick or in prison? In fact, each time they had cared for 'one of the least of these', they were caring for Jesus.

We have been discovering that we cannot simply exploit everything around us for our own benefit. We are becoming aware that we are simply one part of a complex web of life that must be sustained and nurtured, and that our own lives depend on the health of the whole of creation. We cannot simply exercise dominion over creation! Perhaps we can extend Jesus' parable of the sheep and the goats to include our equine brothers and sisters. Rescuing horses, mules and donkeys from cruelty and servitude is as much for our sake as it is for theirs. It begins to put us in a right relationship with God's creation. 'When did we see you suffering?'

Prayers of Recognition

When we have exploited the natural world without thought,
when we have taken without regard for the consequences,
when we have been heedless to cruelty to animals,
(Silence)

Lord, have mercy upon us.
Lord, have mercy upon us.

When we have witnessed human need, poverty, homelessness, despair,
when we have not shared from our plenty,
when we have walked past on the other side,
(Silence)

Christ, have mercy upon us.
Christ, have mercy upon us.

When we have failed to recognize your image in one another,
when we do not recognize your presence in creation,
when we forget that we are creatures like all other creatures,
(silence)

Lord, have mercy upon us.
Lord, have mercy upon us.

May God who gave the horse its might and mane,
who gave creation its life and freedom to become what it may,
forgive us now for our exploitation of the created world.
Give us grace to move from patterns of exploitation
towards a mutual partnership with our horses
and with all our fellow creatures.
May God give us eyes to see, to recognize his presence in all those
    around us:
in the poor, the hungry, the sick and those in prison,
and especially in the face of his Son, Jesus.
Amen.

Blessing of Horses

God who created the natural world,
who called all creatures into existence
and saw that it was all very good,
may your blessing rest upon these horses:
the blessing of shelter and pasture,
the blessing of exercise and grooming,
the blessing of companionship, partnership and care,
the blessing of God
be upon you.
Amen.

Hymn – *suggestions*

> All creatures of our God and King, William Henry Draper
>
> Brother, sister, let me serve you, Richard Gillard

Prayers of Intercession

We pray for all who work with horses,
that they may be able to care for them,
providing all that is needed for a healthy life.
(Silence)

All creatures of our God and King,
lift up your voice and with us sing.

We pray for all who work to rescue horses, donkeys and mules
from lives of servitude, neglect or cruelty.
(Silence)

All creatures of our God and King,
lift up your voice and with us sing.

We pray for all veterinary surgeons, nurses and carers
who work to relieve sickness and pain.
(Silence)

All creatures of our God and King,
lift up your voice and with us sing.

We pray for all who support Riding for the Disabled,
enriching lives by providing therapy and fun for those with disabilities.
(Silence)

All creatures of our God and King,
lift up your voice and with us sing.

We pray for all who, like St Martin, recognize human need,
who care for the hungry, the homeless, the sick and imprisoned.
(Silence)

All creatures of our God and King,
lift up your voice and with us sing.

Jesus taught his friends to pray for God's kingdom to come, saying:

Our Father, who art in heaven,
hallowed be thy name;
thy kingdom come;
thy will be done;
on earth as it is in heaven.
Give us this day our daily bread.
And forgive us our trespasses,
as we forgive those who trespass against us.
And lead us not into temptation;
but deliver us from evil.
For thine is the kingdom,
the power and the glory,
for ever and ever.
Amen.

Hymn – *suggestions*

Creation sings! Each plant and tree, Martin Leckebusch

Great is thy faithfulness, Thomas Chisholm

Blessing

In the abundance of God's creative love,
who holds the whole universe in being;
in the name of Jesus the humble king,
who showed us how to love and forgive;
in the power of the Holy Spirit,
who inspires us to live in partnership with all,
may you know God's blessing of life in all its fullness.
Amen.

Light and Dark

Michaelmas – Finding a point of balance around the autumn equinox

Preparation and Invitation

Michaelmas is the festival of St Michael and All Angels and falls on 29 September, close to the autumn equinox (between 21 and 23 September), which marks the point of equal daytime and night. It is one of the quarter days of the year, when rents were paid in the agricultural world, so farmers and farmworkers could be invited to the service. In times past a stubble goose would form part of the rental paid to landowners, so you could follow the service with a shared meal (you could even feature a goose!). For pudding it is traditional to eat Michaelmas pie, made with the last of the blackberries.

You may like to decorate the church with Michaelmas daisies, which are abundant at this time of year.

In the service a Michaelmas bannock will be shared, so you need to ask someone to make some of these loaves. Traditionally the recipe uses equal quantities of barley, rye and oats, and they are made without using any metal implements!

Gathering Music – *suggestion*

Panis angelicus, César Franck

Welcome and Introduction

Today we celebrate the feast of St Michael and All Angels. The church is decorated with Michaelmas daisies. *Aster* is a Greek word meaning star, and these star-like purple flowers remind us of the angelic host, God's celestial messengers. We remember too the autumn equinox, the point of balance when day and night are the same length. From now onwards the nights will draw in as we move towards winter. It is easy to overlook God's messenger angels in our self-sufficient world. It is easy too to forget about the ancient points of balance and change in our non-stop living. Today we invite the angels to guide us as we worship God.

Hymn – *suggestions*

Come let us join our cheerful songs, Isaac Watts

Ye holy angels bright, Richard Baxter and John Hampden Gurney

Opening Psalm

Praise the Lord!
Praise the Lord from the heavens;
praise him in the heights!
Praise him, all his angels; praise him, all his host!
Praise him, sun and moon;
praise him, all you shining stars!
Praise him, you highest heavens,
and you waters above the heavens!
Let them praise the name of the Lord,
for he commanded and they were created.
He established them for ever and ever;
he fixed their bounds, which cannot be passed.
Praise the Lord!
Psalm 148.1–6

Bible Reading – *Genesis 18.1–8*

The Lord appeared to Abraham by the oaks of Mamre, as he sat at the entrance of his tent in the heat of the day. He looked up and saw three men standing near him. When he saw them, he ran from the tent entrance to meet them, and bowed down to the ground. He said, 'My lord, if I find favour with you, do not pass by your servant. Let a little water be brought, and wash your feet, and rest yourselves under the tree. Let me bring a little bread, that you may refresh yourselves, and after that you may pass on – since you have come to your servant.' So they said, 'Do as you have said.' And Abraham hastened into the tent to Sarah, and said, 'Make ready quickly three measures of choice flour, knead it, and make cakes.' Abraham ran to the herd, and took a calf, tender and good, and gave it to the servant, who hastened to prepare it. Then he took curds and milk and the calf that he had prepared, and set it before them; and he stood by them under the tree while they ate.

Living Word of God,
live in our lives today.

Reflection

When three strangers come near to his camp, Abraham offers them hospitality, inviting them to rest from the heat of the day and share a meal with him. His welcome and generosity are rewarded when the strangers bless him with a promise that he and Sarah will have a long hoped-for child. After the encounter Abraham realizes that he has, in the words of the letter to the Hebrews, been 'entertaining angels unawares'. Abraham's grandson Jacob also experiences angels; one even wrestles with him all night (Genesis 32.22–32)! How many of these chance encounters do we miss because we are too preoccupied with our own concerns? How often do we make time for really encountering the people we see around us, people we often fail properly to notice? Sometimes we are disappointed when prayers seem not to be answered, but it may be that we are simply too busy to notice the messenger angel that God sends. In this next invocation we recognize the watchers and holy ones who surround us and help us.

Invocation to the Angels

Michael, Archangel, who cast down Lucifer,
inspire us to stand with you, against all evil.
You behold him face to face.

Wrestler, who struggled with Jacob through the night,
contend with us, that we may be strengthened.
You behold him face to face.

Gabriel, who called Mary to be the mother of Jesus,
overshadow us with God's power.
You behold him face to face.

Watcher, guardian angel who looks on the face of God,
hold us in your protective gaze.
You behold him face to face.

May God's messenger angels minister to us now
as they ministered to Jesus in the wilderness.
Amen.

Hymn – *suggestions*

Ye watchers and ye holy ones, Athelstan Riley

How shall I sing that majesty, John Mason

Bible Reading – *John 1.47–51*

When Jesus saw Nathanael coming toward him, he said of him, 'Here
is truly an Israelite in whom there is no deceit!' Nathanael asked him,
'Where did you get to know me?' Jesus answered, 'I saw you under
the fig tree before Philip called you.' Nathanael replied, 'Rabbi, you
are the Son of God! You are the King of Israel!' Jesus answered, 'Do
you believe because I told you that I saw you under the fig tree? You
will see greater things than these.' And he said to him, 'Very truly, I
tell you, you will see heaven opened and the angels of God ascending
and descending upon the Son of Man.'

Living Word of God,
live in our lives today.

Reflection

And Jesus said to him, 'Very truly, I tell you, you will see heaven opened and the angels of God ascending and descending upon the Son of Man.' Angels represent that moment of seeing heaven opened, of seeing through the demanding and dominant noise of our everyday lives, through to a deeper reality, a more hidden one. To see heaven opened we need to make space in our lives and our hearts to notice. The thin places where heaven and earth come close are everywhere, if only we can notice them. The point of balance between light and darkness at the equinox reminds us to look for and be attentive to that point of balance in our busy living. In this time of silence, we reflect on where our lives are out of balance, and we ask what it is we need to do to find that point of balance again.

Silence *(two minutes)*

In the silence we hold these questions:

Where is your life out of balance? What needs to change?

Music for Reflection – *suggestion*

Panis angelicus, César Franck

Prayers of Recognition

Where we are sometimes frantic, busy and heedless of so much
    around us,
where we miss the moment of heaven opened,
may we find our point of balance.
(Silence)

May the bread of the Angels
become bread for humankind.

Where we are sometimes caught up only in our own concerns,
our worries, stresses, preoccupations,
where we stop noticing, stop engaging,
may we find our point of balance.
(Silence)

May the bread of the angels
become bread for humankind.

Where we sometimes entertain angels unawares,
failing to recognize your messengers in our midst,
where we try to live only in our own strength,
may we find our point of balance.
(Silence)

May the bread of the angels
become bread for humankind.

Sharing the Michaelmas Bannock

Jesus often called people out into wilderness places, away from the busyness of their lives, to find that point of balance, that thin place where heaven is opened and we can reconnect with God. Michaelmas has traditionally been marked with the sharing of a Michaelmas bannock, a flatbread made from flour from the harvested barley, rye and oats in equal measure. Today we take this 'bread of the angels'. Remembering how Jesus gave thanks, broke the bread and fed the multitude, we share this bread together and give thanks for the blessing of God's messenger angels. So we pray:

As we offer and share this bread of hospitality,
bless us as you blessed Abraham and Sarah.
Help us to recognize your messengers in our midst.
In Jesus' name.
Amen.

The bread is broken and passed from person to person using the words:

May the bread of the angels
become bread for humankind.

Music – *suggestion*

Panis angelicus, César Franck

Hymn – *suggestions*

God himself is present, Gerhard Tersteegen, tr. Frederick W. Foster
Ye servants of the Lord, Philip Doddridge

Prayers of Intercession

We pray for all those who battle with the forces of human greed
   and oppression,
all who stand up against the powers of cruelty or indifference,
all who join with St Michael in the cause of peace, justice and freedom.
(Silence)

He will command his angels concerning you
to guard you in all your ways.
Psalm 91.11

We pray for all who have heard God's call to take a leap of faith,
all who have a sense of vocation to be a channel of God's grace,
for all who sense Gabriel's overshadowing.
(Silence)

He will command his angels concerning you
to guard you in all your ways.

We pray for all who wrestle with the questions of faith and life,
all who struggle with the institutions of religion,
all who hang on and refuse to let go,
all who, like Jacob, grow through the challenge.
(Silence)

He will command his angels concerning you
to guard you in all your ways.

We pray for all who are vulnerable, endangered or in need,
especially children,
that we, with the guardian angels,
may be vigilant in our safeguarding,
daring to speak out and to act when we see abuse or neglect.
(Silence)

He will command his angels concerning you
to guard you in all your ways.

We pray for all those we have loved
who now worship before God's throne,
that great cloud of witnesses
who with all the heavenly host cry out continually,

Holy, Holy, Holy Lord,
God of power and might.
Heaven and earth are full of your glory.
Hosanna in the highest!

We say the Lord's prayer together:

Our Father, who art in heaven,
hallowed be thy name;
thy kingdom come;
thy will be done;
on earth as it is in heaven.
Give us this day our daily bread.
And forgive us our trespasses,
as we forgive those who trespass against us.
And lead us not into temptation;
but deliver us from evil.
For thine is the kingdom,
the power and the glory,
for ever and ever.
Amen.

Hymn – *suggestions*

Praise, my soul, the King of heaven, Henry Francis Lyte

Christ, the fair glory of the holy angels, Rabanus Maurus,
tr. C. S. Phillips

Blessing

God the Father,
send your angels to guard us.
Jesus the Son,
send your angels to guide us.
Spirit of all life,
send your angels to sustain us.
May the blessing of God,
Father, Son and Holy Spirit,
be with us now and as we journey on.
Amen.

OCTOBER

Bread of Community

Harvest Festival – Bringing the whole of ourselves

Preparation and Invitation

Harvest Festival is often the most popular service in the rural calendar for it comes at the culmination of the agricultural year. You may like to invite the farming community as well as those who grow their own food on allotments and in their gardens. Each person could bring an example of their harvest to make a display in church. Sometimes churches use the festival to invite those attending to bring tinned and dried goods to support a local food bank or homeless hostel. Farmers and growers can be invited to take part in the service with readings and prayers.

Each year we recognize an example of where people have gone the extra mile to build up our community life and improve the area for everyone. This might be an environmental project, such as tree planting, species protection, habitat creation; a project to benefit people enjoying the countryside, such as path maintenance, stile repair, organized nature walks; or a project involving children, through a local school or scouts and guide group, helping them to enjoy and respect the countryside. There is an opportunity in the service to interview someone who is making a difference in building up community life, in some way contributing to the common good.

Gathering Music – *suggestion*

Thou visitest the earth, Maurice Greene

Welcome and Introduction

We come to thank God for the harvest, the harvest of our fields and farms, bringing food to our tables and meeting our physical needs. We thank God too for the harvest of our community, our common life together, the harvest of our own deepest selves, our growing towards maturity and wisdom.

Hymn/Song – *suggestions*

Come, ye thankful people, come, Henry Alford

Fill your hearts with joy and gladness, Timothy Dudley-Smith

Opening Psalm

You visit the earth and water it,
you greatly enrich it;
the river of God is full of water;
you provide the people with grain,
for so you have prepared it.
You water its furrows abundantly,
settling its ridges,
softening it with showers,
and blessing its growth.
You crown the year with your bounty;
your wagon tracks overflow with richness.
The pastures of the wilderness overflow,
the hills gird themselves with joy,
the meadows clothe themselves with flocks,
the valleys deck themselves with grain,
they shout and sing together for joy.

Glory to the Father and to the Son and to the Holy Spirit;
as it was in the beginning, is now and shall be for ever. Amen.
Psalm 65.9–13

Reading – 'Seed-Time and Harvest', John Greenleaf Whittier

As o'er his furrowed fields which lie
Beneath a coldly dropping sky,
Yet chill with winter's melted snow,
The husbandman goes forth to sow,

Thus, Freedom, on the bitter blast
The ventures of thy seed we cast,
And trust to warmer sun and rain
To swell the germs and fill the grain.

Who calls thy glorious service hard?
Who deems it not its own reward?
Who, for its trials, counts it less
A cause of praise and thankfulness?

It may not be our lot to wield
The sickle in the ripened field;
Nor ours to hear, on summer eves,
The reaper's song among the sheaves.

Yet where our duty's task is wrought
In unison with God's great thought,
The near and future blend in one,
And whatsoe'er is willed, is done!

And ours the grateful service whence
Comes day by day the recompense;
The hope, the trust, the purpose stayed,
The fountain and the noonday shade.

And were this life the utmost span,
The only end and aim of man,
Better the toil of fields like these
Than waking dream and slothful ease.

But life, though falling like our grain,
Like that revives and springs again;
And, early called, how blest are they
Who wait in heaven their harvest-day!

Hymn/Song – *suggestions*

Praise and thanksgiving, Albert F. Bayly

For the fruits of his creation, Fred Pratt Green

Bible Reading – *Ruth 2.1–7*

Now Naomi had a kinsman on her husband's side, a prominent rich man, of the family of Elimelech, whose name was Boaz. And Ruth the Moabite said to Naomi, 'Let me go to the field and glean among the ears of grain, behind someone in whose sight I may find favour.' She said to her, 'Go, my daughter.' So she went. She came and gleaned in the field behind the reapers. As it happened, she came to the part of the field belonging to Boaz, who was of the family of Elimelech. Just then Boaz came from Bethlehem. He said to the reapers, 'The Lord be with you.' They answered, 'The Lord bless you.' Then Boaz said to his servant who was in charge of the reapers, 'To whom does this young woman belong?' The servant who was in charge of the reapers answered, 'She is the Moabite who came back with Naomi from the country of Moab. She said, "Please let me glean and gather among the sheaves behind the reapers." So she came, and she has been on her feet from early this morning until now, without resting even for a moment.'

Living Word of God,
live in our lives today.

Reflection

What is the real harvest that God is looking for? Certainly, the practical task of providing food for the people of the earth is important: without a good harvest we would starve. The Bible also speaks of other kinds of harvests: the harvest of good works; the harvest of our life's work. Jesus called on God, the Lord of the harvest, to send labourers to gather the spiritual harvest of righteousness, the harvest of salvation. However, the story of Ruth offers another insight into the kind of harvest that God values. Boaz is a faithful Jew, following the teaching in Leviticus (19.9–10) not to harvest right to the edges of the fields, not to pick all the grapes, but to leave some for the gleaners, the poor, the strangers, the unemployed, desperate even to pick up the leftovers. This is a harvest of community, including the needy and strangers. Ruth was able to gather enough both for her own needs and for her mother-in-law. Similarly, Ruth brings her whole self to the task of gleaning the harvest. She works hard and impresses the other workers, and her reputation precedes her: Boaz has heard of her faithfulness and loyalty to Naomi. As a foreigner, a migrant worker, Ruth worked to build bridges of trust into her new community. In our own lives, what are the deeper levels of fruitfulness? How are we building up our community by the way we live?

Silence *(two minutes)*

In the silence we hold these questions:

What is your harvest? How are you productive and fruitful?
How does the harvest of your hands build up community and care
   for others?

Prayers of Recognition

We bring to God all that is productive in our lives,
our work in sustaining ourselves, our family and friends,
the satisfaction it brings to us.
(Silence)

We sing the song of harvest home.
All is safely gathered in.

We bring to God all that we do to build up our community,
the taxes we pay, the charities we support,
the time we give freely as we connect with others.
(Silence)

We sing the song of harvest home.
All is safely gathered in.

We bring to God all that we are becoming in our character and
   personality,
the lessons of life we are learning, the weaknesses we are overcoming,
the way we are growing in our faith.
(Silence)

We sing the song of harvest home.
All is safely gathered in.

We also bring to God some of the darker side of our harvests,
the inequality that has grown in our society,
the way we have undervalued some people.
(Silence)

Wheat and tares together sown,
unto joy or sorrow grown.

We bring to God the harvests we know are wrong,
the way we have damaged our planet, taking without heed,
the consumption and waste that we have allowed.
(Silence)

Wheat and tares together sown,
unto joy or sorrow grown.

We bring to God the parts of ourselves that we are ashamed of,
our self-interest and our greed,
our short-term horizon and our narrow vision,
the shallowness of our lives and concerns.
(Silence)

Wheat and tares together sown,
unto joy or sorrow grown.

Assurance of Forgiveness

God, you love us more than we can imagine,
you see us as we truly are,
the wheat and tares of our lives.
You run towards us with outstretched arms
to forgive us and welcome us home.
Give us grace to let go of all that harms us
and to be caught up in the winnowing of your Spirit,
gathering us as one people into the storehouse of your love.
In Jesus' name.
Amen.

Hymn/Song – *suggestions*

Great is thy faithfulness, Thomas Chisholm

Praise, O praise our God and king, Henry Williams Baker

Harvest of our Community – *Interview*

A person representing a community project that is contributing to the common good is interviewed about their work and the difference the project is making.

Hymn/Song – *suggestions*

Lord, we thank you for the promise, Martin E. Leckebusch

Lord, you created a world rich in splendour, Nick Fawcett

Prayers of Intercession

We give thanks for the harvest of the land.
We pray for all who work to bring us the essentials of life.
We remember the challenges of the growing season.
We pray for all who are facing changing times with new priorities.
May we be like Boaz, capable and productive
yet leaving enough for others to live.
(Silence)

Lord of the harvest,
hear our prayer.

We give thanks for the harvest of our community life.
We pray for all who give their time freely to build up our shared life,
to contribute to the common good.
Help us all to think of others and to act for future generations.
May we be like Ruth, working not just for ourselves
but building bridges of trust that cross the boundaries of difference.
(Silence)

Lord of the harvest,
hear our prayer.

We give thanks for the harvest of our own lives,
for all that has been productive and fruitful in us.
Give us grace to grow in wisdom and understanding,
to learn to listen for your voice.
May we be like Boaz and Ruth, who find a new future together,
on the foundation of your love.
(Silence)

Lord of the harvest,
hear our prayer.

We hold in our prayers all who are struggling with illness or disability,
especially those in the farming community,
whose work can have a long-term impact on health.
We remember those who have died
and are gathered into the harvest of heaven.
(Silence)

Lord of the harvest,
hear our prayer.

We say the Lord's prayer together:

Our Father, who art in heaven,
hallowed be thy name;
thy kingdom come;
thy will be done;
on earth as it is in heaven.
Give us this day our daily bread.
And forgive us our trespasses,
as we forgive those who trespass against us.
And lead us not into temptation;
but deliver us from evil.
For thine is the kingdom,
the power and the glory,
for ever and ever.
Amen.

Hymn/Song – *suggestions*

We plough the fields and scatter, Matthias Claudius

To thee, O Lord, our hearts we raise, William Chatterton Dix

Blessing

God of the harvest,
bless the labours of our hearts and hands,
bless the fruits of our cooperation and community,
bless the gathering of neighbours and strangers.
Awaken us to your longing for a different world,
where all are welcomed, valued and appreciated.
Give us grace to discern your presence in one another
and in the invitation of your Son, Jesus Christ,
that, together, we may come to the eternal harvest of your grace.
Amen.

All Creatures of our God

St Francis – Welcoming our animal companions

Francis of Assisi

Preparation and Invitation

You will need to publicize this service in advance, inviting people to bring their pets and animals to church for this celebration. You may like to invite representatives from local veterinary practices, animal charities or groups that work with animals. These people could be invited to take part in readings and prayers in the service. There is an opportunity to interview someone about their work with animals.

Gathering Music – *suggestion*

The Carnival of the Animals – The aquarium, Camille Saint-Saëns

Welcome and Introduction

We come to celebrate the unique relationships we have with our animals. We give thanks to God for the gift of companionship and support that animals provide for so many – from all kinds of pets at home, to highly trained support animals who guide and care for people with a range of conditions and disabilities. Jesus taught us, 'Are not five sparrows sold for two pennies? Yet not one of them is forgotten in

God's sight' (Luke 12.6). God cares for the whole of creation and asks us to do the same. St Francis of Assisi lived from 1181 to 1226 and his feast day is 4 October. He is remembered as a friend of the natural world: birds, animals, sun, moon, stars, calling all of them his brothers and sisters.

Hymn/Song – *suggestions*

All creatures of our God and King, William Henry Draper (after St Francis)

All things bright and beautiful, Cecil Frances Alexander

Opening Prayer

God of all creatures, great and small,
teach us to recognize our connection
in the family of your creation.
Help us to know our interdependence with the world of animals.
Thank you for the comfort and companionship they bring.
We bless you for the wisdom of St Francis of Assisi,
who called them brothers and sisters
and called us to care for them.
In Jesus' name we pray.
Amen.

Opening Psalm

You make springs gush forth in the valleys;
they flow between the hills,
giving drink to every wild animal;
the wild asses quench their thirst.
By the streams the birds of the air have their habitation;
they sing among the branches.
From your lofty abode you water the mountains;
the earth is satisfied with the fruit of your work.
You cause the grass to grow for the cattle,
and plants for people to use,
to bring forth food from the earth,
and wine to gladden the human heart,
oil to make the face shine,
and bread to strengthen the human heart.

The trees of the Lord are watered abundantly,
the cedars of Lebanon that he planted.
In them the birds build their nests;
the stork has its home in the fir trees.
The high mountains are for the wild goats;
the rocks are a refuge for the coneys.

Glory to the Father and to the Son and to the Holy Spirit;
as it was in the beginning, is now and shall be for ever. Amen.
Psalm 104.10–18

Reading – The Little Flowers of St Francis of Assisi, *chapter 21, tr. Roger Hudleston*

At the time when St Francis was living in the city of Gubbio, a large
wolf appeared in the neighbourhood, so terrible and so fierce, that
he not only devoured other animals, but made a prey of men also;
and since he often approached the town, all the people were in great
alarm, and used to go about armed, as if going to battle. Notwith-
standing these precautions, if any of the inhabitants ever met him
alone, he was sure to be devoured, as all defence was useless: and,
through fear of the wolf, they dared not go beyond the city walls. St
Francis, feeling great compassion for the people of Gubbio, resolved
to go and meet the wolf, though all advised him not to do so. Making the sign of the holy cross, and putting all his confidence in God,
he went forth from the city, taking his brethren with him; but these
fearing to go any further, St Francis bent his steps alone toward the
spot where the wolf was known to be, while many people followed
at a distance, and witnessed the miracle. The wolf, seeing all this
multitude, ran towards St Francis with his jaws wide open. As he
approached, the saint, making the sign of the cross, cried out: 'Come
hither, brother wolf; I command thee, in the name of Christ, neither
to harm me nor anybody else.' Marvellous to tell, no sooner had St
Francis made the sign of the cross, than the terrible wolf, closing his
jaws, stopped running, and coming up to St Francis, lay down at his
feet as meekly as a lamb.

Reflection

The stories of St Francis preaching to the birds, or negotiating with
a wolf, might be highly imaginative but they reflect a deeper truth in
his life: a respect and care for animal life and a recognition of how

much we share as creatures. St Francis said, 'If you have men who will exclude any of God's creatures from the shelter of compassion and pity, you will have men who will deal likewise with their fellow men.' There is a continuity between how we honour animal life and how we treat our human neighbours. Going further, the prophet Isaiah envisioned a future where 'The wolf shall live with the lamb, the leopard shall lie down with the kid, the calf and the lion and the fatling together, and a little child shall lead them' (Isaiah 11.6). We live in a time of unprecedented extinction, where human beings have only been concerned for their own needs. We are discovering that without 'brother wolf', many ecosystems collapse. We belong together, in the complex web of life.

Hymn/Song – *suggestions*

> Make me a channel of your peace, Sebastian Temple (after St Francis)
>
> Dance and sing all the earth, John L. Bell and Graham Maule

Bible Reading – *Job 12.7–13*

> But ask the animals, and they will teach you; the birds of the air, and they will tell you; ask the plants of the earth, and they will teach you; and the fish of the sea will declare to you. Who among all these does not know that the hand of the Lord has done this? In his hand is the life of every living thing and the breath of every human being. Does not the ear test words as the palate tastes food? Is wisdom with the aged, and understanding in length of days? With God are wisdom and strength; he has counsel and understanding.

Living Word of God,
live in our lives today.

Silence *(two minutes)*

In the silence we hold these questions:

What does your relationship with animals mean to you?
What have you learned from that relationship?

Music for Reflection – *suggestion*

> *The Carnival of the Animals* – The aquarium, Camille Saint-Saëns

Conversation

We turn to a neighbour and explore what our animals mean to us and why we form such deep bonds with them.

Interview

A local vet or someone who is involved with animal care is interviewed about their work. The discussion may include a focus on what animals have to teach us and what we can learn form our animals.

Hymn/Song – *suggestions*

O God, your creatures fill the earth, Carolyn Winfrey Gillette

Creation sings, Martin E. Leckebusch

The Blessing of Animals

The service leader moves around the gathering to those who have brought animals, asks the animal's name and gives thanks for them.

Brother/Sister [Name],
We thank God for you,
for the unique gift of your presence,
to remind us of our shared place in the web of life.
May God who made you, bless you now.
Thanks be to God.

Prayers of Intercession

We give thanks for the gift of animal companions:
our pets, for all that alleviate loneliness,
giving comfort and reassurance.
We pray for all who care for animals,
for veterinary staff and animal sanctuaries.
(Silence)

Lord of creation,
hear our prayer.

We give thanks for close working partnerships with animals:
for animals in security and in medicine, helping us by their acute senses;
for those who lead and protect people with impaired faculties.
We pray for all who train and care for these working animals.
(Silence)

Lord of creation,
hear our prayer.

We pray for all who seek to protect animals,
those that have been abused or abandoned,
those bred in poor conditions for profit.
We pray for the work of the RSPCA and all animal charities.
(Silence)

Lord of creation,
hear our prayer.

We think of those animals we have known and loved,
for long lives of loyal companionship,
or lives suddenly cut short by illness or accident.
We give thanks for the many blessings our pets have brought us.
(Silence)

Lord of creation,
hear our prayer.

We say the Lord's prayer together:

Our Father, who art in heaven,
hallowed be thy name;
thy kingdom come;
thy will be done;
on earth as it is in heaven.
Give us this day our daily bread.
And forgive us our trespasses,
as we forgive those who trespass against us.
And lead us not into temptation;
but deliver us from evil.
For thine is the kingdom,
the power and the glory,
for ever and ever.
Amen.

Hymn/Song – *suggestions*

O Lord of every shining constellation, Albert F. Bayly

Lord of creation, to you be all praise, Jack C. Winslow

Blessing

God of all creatures,
bless us now in our care for creation.
Jesus who counted the sparrows,
bless us now as we notice all who share our world.
Spirit who comes as a dove,
bless us now as we seek your peace.
May God bless us,
Father, Son and Holy Spirit.
Amen.

NOVEMBER

The Light of Life

All Souls – Remembering loved ones

All Souls Day

Preparation and Invitation

Families who have been bereaved in the past year can be invited to attend this service as an opportunity to remember their loved ones. We have had higher levels of response from handwritten invitations than from printed ones – the more personal a letter can be, the more likely people are to attend.

*You will need to prepare a place in the church for people to come to light candles – either a votive candle stand if you already have one, or you can use a sand tray with tealights. It is **very important** that you do not have the candles too close together, as they can suddenly ignite all together as they become hot. It is wise to have a fire blanket nearby, and somebody briefed to watch and be prepared to act in an emergency.*

You will also need some people available to welcome the congregation and help identify those hoping to light a candle. We have small cards available so that people can write down the names of those they wish to remember. They bring the card with them at the time of remembrance, passing it to a reader, who reads out the name as the mourners move forward to light a candle. We usually have two more helpers at the candle stand to assist people as they are lighting candles.

Gathering Music – *suggestion*

When David heard, Eric Whitacre

Welcome and Introduction

The feast of All Souls is a traditional time for us to remember those we have loved who have died. It comes as a marker in the year, a stepping stone in the process of grieving, where we can name and commemorate our dead. Today we come together all knowing what it is to grieve. We will invite you to come and light a candle of remembrance as we name the person you have lost, and as we take hold of God's promise of eternal life for each one of us.

Hymn/Song – *suggestions*

Be still for the presence of the Lord, David J. Evans

The Lord's my shepherd, Stuart Townend

Opening Prayer

God of compassion,
you are close to the broken-hearted.
You draw near to all who mourn.
Hear us as we call to you now.
Bind up our wounds.
Touch us with your healing grace as we grieve.
Hold in your arms of love all who have died,
all whose memory we treasure.
We ask in the name of Jesus,
who wept at the grave of his friend Lazarus
and who weeps with us now.
Amen.

There is real honesty, a raw grief expressed in the following psalm. It is bleak and uncompromising, it doesn't sugar the pill, and that can be helpful to us who grieve today.

Opening Psalm

Be gracious to me, O Lord, for I am in distress;
my eye wastes away from grief,
my soul and body also.
For my life is spent with sorrow,
and my years with sighing;
my strength fails because of my misery,
and my bones waste away.
I am the scorn of all my adversaries,
a horror to my neighbours,
an object of dread to my acquaintances;
those who see me in the street flee from me.
I have passed out of mind like one who is dead;
I have become like a broken vessel.

Glory to the Father and to the Son and to the Holy Spirit;
as it was in the beginning, is now and shall be for ever. Amen.
Psalm 31.9–12

Reading – *2 Samuel 18.31–33*

Then the Cushite came; and the Cushite said, 'Good tidings for my lord the king! For the Lord has vindicated you this day, delivering you from the power of all who rose up against you.' The king said to the Cushite, 'Is it well with the young man Absalom?' The Cushite answered, 'May the enemies of my lord the king, and all who rise up to do you harm, be like that young man.'

The king was deeply moved, and went up to the chamber over the gate, and wept; and as he went, he said, 'O my son Absalom, my son, my son Absalom! Would I had died instead of you, O Absalom, my son, my son!'

Living Word of God,
live in our lives today.

Reflection

Absalom had worked to usurp his father, King David, and a battle had been fought in which Absalom had been killed. Despite their differences, David was overwhelmed with grief on the news of his son's death. This is possibly the most anguished scene of grief in the Bible.

When David cries out, 'O my son Absalom, my son, my son Absalom!', he is absolutely heartbroken. Like any parent who has seen their own child die before them he wishes it could have been him instead. 'Would I had died instead of you, O Absalom, my son, my son!'

We have become embarrassed at outward expressions of grief. Our society has become uncomfortable with death. It is left to the professionals. We are granted some compassionate leave and then we are expected to get on with life. Perhaps the Victorians were more realistic, with their mourning rituals and practices. The feelings can be overwhelming, and they need to be expressed: tears need to be shed, pain released. Healthy grief can take years to work through, not months or weeks. Stepping stones, milestones, key personal dates and anniversaries – all are important, as is a time like this. In time, happier memories can surface again and we can begin to move on. We can picture God, the loving Father, welcoming our loved ones home into an eternal embrace of love. Eric Whitacre wrote his choral work 'When David heard' for a friend who had lost his son. It can give us some space to reflect on where we are on our own journey of grief.

Silence

In the silence we hold these questions:

Where am I on my journey of grief?
Numb, cold, disbelieving? Angry or feeling guilty? Accepting, adapting, coping?
Relieved, thankful, at peace?

Music for Reflection – *suggestion*

When David heard, Eric Whitacre

Prayers of Recognition

We bring to God the pain, sorrow and grief of our loss.
We bring the painful memories, the regrets and fears,
knowing that Jesus weeps with us.
(Silence)

Come to me, all who are heavy laden,
and I will give you rest.

We bring to God the ways we have tried to avoid the hurt,
the distractions and diversions, the attempts to numb the pain,
knowing that Jesus weeps with us.
(Silence)

Come to me, all who are heavy laden,
and I will give you rest.

We bring to God the responses of others,
the kindness and good intentions,
the avoidance and misunderstanding,
knowing that Jesus weeps with us.
(Silence)

Come to me, all who are heavy laden,
and I will give you rest.

Hymn/Song – *suggestions*

Take this moment, sign, and space, John L. Bell

There's a wideness in God's mercy, Frederick William Faber

Bible Reading – *John 11.17–27*

When Jesus arrived, he found that Lazarus had already been in the tomb four days. Now Bethany was near Jerusalem, some two miles away, and many of the Jews had come to Martha and Mary to console them about their brother. When Martha heard that Jesus was coming, she went and met him, while Mary stayed at home. Martha said to Jesus, 'Lord, if you had been here, my brother would not have died. But even now I know that God will give you whatever you ask of him.' Jesus said to her, 'Your brother will rise again.' Martha said to him, 'I know that he will rise again in the resurrection on the last day.' Jesus said to her, 'I am the resurrection and the life. Those who believe in me, even though they die, will live, and everyone who lives and believes in me will never die. Do you believe this?' She said to him, 'Yes, Lord, I believe that you are the Messiah, the Son of God, the one coming into the world.'

Living Word of God,
live in our lives today.

Reflection

Elsewhere in this passage Jesus is deeply moved by the grief of his friends, Martha and Mary, as they mourn the loss of their brother Lazarus. He weeps with them. You can hear the echoes of blame that hang in the air: 'if you had been here' he would not have died. But alongside the tears and sorrow there is a deep faith that even in this tragedy they are held in the hope of the resurrection. Jesus goes one step further and says, 'I am the resurrection and the life', promising that life for all who believe in him. This is the faith we proclaim today as we light a candle of remembrance: that 'everyone who lives and believes in me will never die'.

Candles of Remembrance

We are invited to come forward to bring the names of our loved ones and to light candles of remembrance.

Music – *suggestion*

O magnum mysterium, Morten Lauridsen

Hymn/Song – *suggestions*

From the falter of breath, John L. Bell and Graham Maule

O love that wilt not let me go, George Matheson

Prayers of Intercession

We pray for one another and all who have been bereaved.
We give thanks for those who have helped and supported us in our
    journey of grief.
(Silence)

Hear us, good Lord,
healer of the broken-hearted.

We pray for parents who have lost a child
and for all who have had to face unexpected, untimely death.
(Silence)

Hear us, good Lord,
healer of the broken-hearted.

We pray for those who have been living with dementia
and the slow loss of connection with others this can bring.
(Silence)

Hear us, good Lord,
healer of the broken-hearted.

We pray for those who have died violently or accidentally,
and for the shock and trauma that this can bring.
(Silence)

Hear us, good Lord,
healer of the broken-hearted.

We commend all those who have died
into the arms and the love of God,
knowing that in that embrace all shall be made well,
all hurts will be healed, all will be made whole,
and in that love we shall one day be reunited.
Through Jesus who died, was buried,
and who rose again, for us.
Amen.

We say the Lord's prayer together:

Our Father, who art in heaven,
hallowed be thy name;
thy kingdom come;
thy will be done;
on earth as it is in heaven.
Give us this day our daily bread.
And forgive us our trespasses,
as we forgive those who trespass against us.
And lead us not into temptation;
but deliver us from evil.
For thine is the kingdom,
the power and the glory,
for ever and ever.
Amen.

Hymn/Song – *suggestions*

Now thank we all our God, Martin Rinkart, tr. Catherine Winkworth

Dear Lord and Father of mankind, John Greenleaf Whittier

Blessing

God of all compassion,
hold us now in your fierce love.
Son of God who gave his life for us,
hold us now in your resurrection promise.
Holy Spirit who comforts us,
hold us now in your deep peace.
May the blessing of God,
Father, Son and Holy Spirit,
be with us now and for ever.
Amen.

Rockets and Sparklers

All Saints – Not hiding our lights

Preparation and Invitation

You will need some indoor sparklers, enough for each person – or some nominated representatives – to light one during the act of commitment. Have a bucket of water nearby to dispose of the exhausted sparklers.

Gathering Music – *suggestion*

Music for the Royal Fireworks, George Frideric Handel

Welcome and Introduction

All Saints' Day falls on 1 November – a time when the sky at night is often full of fireworks for Bonfire Night or Diwali. These explosions of light in the darkness remind us of the heroes of our faith, the saints, whose lives lit up the darkness of their own time. Some saints are like rockets, high-fliers, famed through time, remembered by name. Many more are like sparklers, bringing light to those around them, but they may never be widely recognized. Today we come to remember them all and to ask how we may be called to be saints and to bring light in our time.

Hymn/Song – *suggestions*

Who are these like stars appearing, Heinrich Schenck, tr. Frances Elizabeth Cox

Ye watchers and ye holy ones, Athelstan Riley

Opening Prayer

God of light,
you have called your saints in every age
to live lives of transparent integrity,
to be honest in their faults and failings,
to be open in their weakness and vulnerability,
that your all-sufficient grace may shine through them.
Inspire us now to follow your saints in faith and hope.
Shine through our living with your one true light,
revealed in Jesus Christ your Son.
Amen.

Opening Responses

Now faith is the assurance of things hoped for,
the conviction of things not seen.
Indeed, by faith our ancestors received approval.
By faith we understand that the worlds were prepared by the word of God,
so that what is seen
was made from things that are not visible.
Hebrews 11.1–3

Bible Reading – *Hebrews 12.1–2*

Therefore, since we are surrounded by so great a cloud of witnesses, let us also lay aside every weight and the sin that clings so closely, and let us run with perseverance the race that is set before us, looking to Jesus the pioneer and perfecter of our faith, who for the sake of the joy that was set before him endured the cross, disregarding its shame, and has taken his seat at the right hand of the throne of God.

Living Word of God,
live in our lives today.

Prayers of Penitence

We bring to God the heavy burdens of guilt and regret that we carry,
the words and actions we wish we could undo.
(Silence)

Let us lay aside every weight.
Let us run with perseverance.

We bring to God the times when we lose our motivation,
times when we feel apathetic or lacking in energy.
(Silence)

Let us lay aside every weight.
Let us run with perseverance.

We bring to God our lack of confidence,
the times we do not believe in ourselves or our calling.
(Silence)

Let us lay aside every weight.
Let us run with perseverance.

Lord Jesus,
the pioneer and perfecter of our faith,
as we turn to you and lay our burdens down,
set us free from all guilt and regret,
from all that undermines us,
that we may run the race you have set before us,
in the confidence of your calling,
to be your saints.
Amen.

Hymn/Song – *suggestions*

Rejoice in God's saints, Fred Pratt Green

Praise to God for saints and martyrs, Michael Forster

Bible Reading – *Matthew 5.1–12*

When Jesus saw the crowds, he went up the mountain; and after he sat down, his disciples came to him. Then he began to speak, and taught them, saying:

'Blessed are the poor in spirit, for theirs is the kingdom of heaven.

'Blessed are those who mourn, for they will be comforted.

'Blessed are the meek, for they will inherit the earth.

'Blessed are those who hunger and thirst for righteousness, for they will be filled.

'Blessed are the merciful, for they will receive mercy.

'Blessed are the pure in heart, for they will see God.

'Blessed are the peacemakers, for they will be called children of God.

'Blessed are those who are persecuted for righteousness' sake, for theirs is the kingdom of heaven.

'Blessed are you when people revile you and persecute you and utter all kinds of evil against you falsely on my account. Rejoice and be glad, for your reward is great in heaven, for in the same way they persecuted the prophets who were before you.'

Living Word of God,
live in our lives today.

Reflection

Most of us will not be like rockets, lighting up the sky for miles around. More likely we will be sparklers, living lives that can bring light on a more modest scale. Celebrity and popularity can be very distorting, and Jesus brings the life of faith right down to earth in the Beatitudes. Those who are blessed are ordinary people, doing their best to live lives of love in difficult circumstances. The poor in spirit, those who mourn, the meek, those who long for a better world, the merciful, the pure, the peacemakers and those who are persecuted – all these are God's everyday saints! And we are caught up in that great cloud of witnesses, not because of our own qualities or goodness but because we have been called to bear witness to God's grace and presence in our lives. We are simply the windows through which God's light can shine.

Silence *(two minutes)*

In the silence we hold these questions:

Where do you feel you are in the list of those who Jesus called blessed?
How can you allow God to shine through your living?

Music for Reflection – *suggestion*

The Planets – Venus, the bringer of peace, Gustav Holst

Prayers of Recognition

We bring to God the challenges we face in our lives,
the least likely parts of ourselves to feel blessed.
(Silence)

You show me the path of life.
In your presence there is fullness of joy.
Psalm 16.11

We bring to God the weaknesses we perceive in our character,
the least likely parts of ourselves to feel blessed.
(Silence)

You show me the path of life.
In your presence there is fullness of joy.

We bring to God our true selves, warts and all,
the least likely parts of ourselves to feel blessed.
(Silence)

You show me the path of life.
In your presence there is fullness of joy.

Act of Commitment

We say together:

We are God's saints!
We are witnesses to Jesus!
We are windows for the Holy Spirit to shine through!

We offer our lives afresh today, to be filled with God's life and love.
Amen.

We light an indoor sparkler to celebrate our calling.

Music – *suggestion*

Music for the Royal Fireworks, George Frideric Handel

Hymn/Song – *suggestions*

Adoramus te, Domine, Taizé Community

O Lord, hear our prayer, Taizé Community

Prayers of Intercession

We give thanks for the heroes of our faith,
famous men and women whose lives are celebrated today.
We pray for those who live in the public gaze,
celebrities, leaders of the nations,
that they may find ways of living authentically.
(Silence)

As we join with all your saints,
hear our prayer.

We give thanks for that great cloud of witnesses,
known only to you, whose names are not remembered
yet whose lives lit up the darkness of their time.
We pray for those who are overlooked or unnoticed today,
those who maintain the fabric of this world unseen.
(Silence)

As we join with all your saints,
hear our prayer.

We give thanks for those who have inspired us in our own lives,
those who by their example have shown us
a living faith, a better way to live.
We pray for our own lives, the way we live,
that we may touch others as we shine with the light of your love.
(Silence)

As we join with all your saints,
hear our prayer.

We give you thanks for those who stand up to be counted,
those who campaign for others,
those who defend the vulnerable.
We pray for all who suffer for their faith,
all prisoners of conscience.
We pray for the work of Amnesty International in seeking
   their freedom.
(Silence)

As we join with all your saints,
hear our prayer.

We hold before you all who are struggling
with chronic illness, pain or disability.
We pray for all carers, especially young carers,
who give their lives to support others.
(Silence)

As we join with all your saints,
hear our prayer.

We remember all who have died,
commending them to the love and mercy of God,
in company with all the saints,
that great cloud of witnesses
who surround us when we pray.
(Silence)

As we join with all your saints,
hear our prayer.

We say the Lord's prayer together:

**Our Father, who art in heaven,
hallowed be thy name;
thy kingdom come;
thy will be done;
on earth as it is in heaven.
Give us this day our daily bread.**

And forgive us our trespasses,
as we forgive those who trespass against us.
And lead us not into temptation;
but deliver us from evil.
For thine is the kingdom,
the power and the glory,
for ever and ever.
Amen.

Hymn/Song – *suggestions*

For all the saints, William Walsham How

Disposer supreme, Jean-Baptiste de Santeuil, tr. Isaac Williams

Blessing

Holy God,
you call us to be holy,
bless us in our weakness.
Incarnate Word,
you show us how to be human,
bless us in our becoming.
Holy Spirit,
you dwell in our hearts,
bless us with your encouraging presence.
May God bless us,
with all the saints,
Father, Son and Holy Spirit.
Amen.

DECEMBER

Jesse Tree

Advent –Deep roots preparing the way

Preparation and Invitation

This service could be used in several ways: as a family service for Advent Sunday; as a school service during Advent; or as a service to be used at home during Advent.

Lots of people enjoy researching into their family history and making a family tree. Here is an opportunity to make one for Jesus. You could invite a group of children, perhaps from the church or a local school, to produce the symbols to be hung on the Jesse Tree. Many sources of printable images are available on the internet, or a more creative process might be to invite the children to plan and produce the symbols themselves. Images are available from http://images.rca.org/docs/resources/JesseTreeornaments3inch.pdf.

You will need a suitable tree to hang the images on, set up on a steady base. Some people use a bare branch, others a conifer or other evergreen tree. Alternatively, you could use a two-dimensional picture of a tree that the symbols could be fixed to.

Children could be invited to be involved in reading and praying in the service.

Depending on the length of service that you want to plan, you could replace the Bible readings with some shorter summaries of each character, or you could reduce the number of characters that you include.

Gathering Music – *suggestion*

Look at the world, John Rutter

Welcome and Introduction

We all know the Christmas story, about Mary and Joseph, the inn-keeper, the shepherds and a baby born in a stable. But why did it all happen? Today we are going to discover the whole story, of how our world went all wrong. We will trace the journey and find out about the people who prepared the way for the promised Saviour. We will hear how God came to save us – came in person, as Jesus the child of Beth-lehem. We will be building a Jesse Tree, because of an ancient prophecy that a shoot would grow out of the stump of Jesse. Jesse was the father of King David and was one of the people preparing the way for Jesus.

Opening Prayer

Loving God,
you created the world and all of us,
to live in peace and harmony,
to live in balance with nature,
to live life in all its fullness.
Yet we have chosen other ways,
we have damaged our world,
we have hurt one another,
we have lost our way.
In this Jesse Tree
we trace the story of your loving plan
to bring us home to you.
Be with us now as we gather in your name.
Amen.

Hymn/Song – *suggestions*

He's got the whole world in his hands, Traditional

How lovely on the mountains, Leonard E. Smith

Opening Responses

A shoot shall come out from the stump of Jesse,
and a branch shall grow out of his roots.

The spirit of the Lord shall rest on him,
the spirit of wisdom and understanding,
the spirit of counsel and might,
the spirit of knowledge and the fear of the Lord.
Isaiah 11.1–2

Adam and Eve – making choices

Bible Reading – *Genesis 1.26–27*

Then God said, 'Let us make humankind in our image, according to our likeness; and let them have dominion over the fish of the sea, and over the birds of the air, and over the cattle, and over all the wild animals of the earth, and over every creeping thing that creeps upon the earth.' So God created humankind in his image, in the image of God he created them; male and female he created them.

Reflection

It all began in a garden with the first human family: God's longing for those who could love and laugh, create and discover, made in God's image and likeness. But to be free to love we had to be free to choose, to choose to love rather than to hate, to choose light instead of darkness, to choose right before wrong. We made the wrong choices; we spoiled the garden. Adam and Eve remind us of the goodness of creation and the balance of nature. How can we find that again?

Prayer

God of love, help us to learn the ways of love.
God of light, help us to find you in the darkness.
God of right, where we go wrong, help us to find your way,
through Jesus, who is the shoot from the stump of Jesse.
Amen.

The symbol for Adam and Eve is hung on the Jesse Tree.

Abraham and Sarah – a call and a promise

Bible Reading – *Genesis 15.1–6*

After these things, the word of the Lord came to Abram in a vision, 'Do not be afraid, Abram, I am your shield; your reward shall be very great.' But Abram said, 'O Lord God, what will you give me, for I continue childless, and the heir of my house is Eliezer of Damascus?' And Abram said, 'You have given me no offspring, and so a slave born in my house is to be my heir.' But the word of the Lord came to him, 'This man shall not be your heir; no one but your very own issue shall be your heir.' He brought him outside and said, 'Look towards heaven and count the stars, if you are able to count them.' Then he said to him, 'So shall your descendants be.' And he believed the Lord; and the Lord reckoned it to him as righteousness.

Reflection

God had called Abram and his wife Sarai to leave behind everything and to journey into the unknown, to become a new people, the people of God. God gave Abram a new name, Abraham, and his wife became Sarah. They longed for a child, but it seemed impossible. God told Abraham to look up at the sky and promised him as many descendants as there were stars! God has begun the long journey towards us. How can we turn to meet God?

Prayer

God of faith, help us to learn the ways of faith.
God of hope, help us to believe your promises.
God who calls, help us to leave the past behind and to follow you,
through Jesus, who is the shoot from the stump of Jesse.
Amen.

The symbol for Abraham and Sarah is hung on the Jesse Tree.

Hymn/Song – *suggestions*

God it was who said to Abraham, John L. Bell and Graham Maule

One more step along the world, Sydney Carter

Jacob's Ladder – wrestling with angels

Bible Reading – *Genesis 28.10–13, 16–17*

Jacob left Beer-sheba and went towards Haran. He came to a certain place and stayed there for the night, because the sun had set. Taking one of the stones of the place, he put it under his head and lay down in that place. And he dreamed that there was a ladder set up on the earth, the top of it reaching to heaven; and the angels of God were ascending and descending on it. And the Lord stood beside him and said, 'I am the Lord, the God of Abraham your father and the God of Isaac; the land on which you lie I will give to you and to your offspring.' Then Jacob woke from his sleep and said, 'Surely the Lord is in this place – and I did not know it!' And he was afraid, and said, 'How awesome is this place! This is none other than the house of God, and this is the gate of heaven.'

Reflection

Jacob made some rotten choices. He was a runaway and a cheat, but despite his bad start he became a great leader. One story tells of how Jacob wrestled with an angel, and against the odds hung on to his opponent until daybreak. He was wrestling with what kind of a person he would become. In this dream, Jacob sees a ladder into heaven; he realizes that God has a purpose for him, and that God is with us wherever we go, even when we go wrong! God gave him a new name: Israel. A new name and a new beginning. How can we make a new start in our lives?

Prayer

God of our wrestling, help us to hang on to you.
God of our dreaming, lift our eyes to see you all around us.
God of new beginnings, help us to grow into the people we could be,
through Jesus, who is the shoot from the stump of Jesse.
Amen.

The symbol for Jacob is hung on the Jesse Tree.

Joseph's Coat – making the best of it

Bible Reading – *Genesis 37.2–4*

> Joseph, being seventeen years old, was shepherding the flock with
> his brothers; he was a helper to the sons of Bilhah and Zilpah, his
> father's wives; and Joseph brought a bad report of them to their
> father. Now Israel loved Joseph more than any other of his children,
> because he was the son of his old age; and he had made him a long
> robe with sleeves. But when his brothers saw that their father loved
> him more than all his brothers, they hated him, and could not speak
> peaceably to him.

Reflection

I wonder if Joseph's father, Jacob, should have had a favourite son.
It's not really surprising his brothers were resentful. Joseph was given
a special long-sleeved coat, and he had dreams about being famous
and important. It led to all sorts of trouble. His brothers sold Joseph
as a slave into Egypt and he ended up in prison, but his dreams helped
Pharaoh to prepare for a long famine. Joseph's family came to Egypt
to find food and they were reunited, and he forgave them. God taught
him how to make the best of a bad situation. He had to have faith. Can
we learn to trust God, even when things go wrong?

Prayer

God, you have no favourites, you love us equally.
Help us to trust in you when things go wrong.
Help us to have faith that you will bring us through safely,
through Jesus, who is the shoot from the stump of Jesse.
Amen.

The symbol for Joseph is hung on the Jesse Tree.

Hymn/Song – *suggestions*

As Jacob with travel was weary one day, Harry Loper

God is love: his the care, Percy Dearmer

Moses the Liberator – longing for freedom

Bible Reading – *Exodus 3.1–5, 7–8*

Moses was keeping the flock of his father-in-law Jethro, the priest of
Midian; he led his flock beyond the wilderness, and came to Horeb,
the mountain of God. There the angel of the Lord appeared to him in
a flame of fire out of a bush; he looked, and the bush was blazing, yet
it was not consumed. Then Moses said, 'I must turn aside and look
at this great sight, and see why the bush is not burned up.' When the
Lord saw that he had turned aside to see, God called to him out of the
bush, 'Moses, Moses!' And he said, 'Here I am.' Then he said, 'Come
no closer! Remove the sandals from your feet, for the place on which
you are standing is holy ground.'

Then the Lord said, 'I have observed the misery of my people who
are in Egypt; I have heard their cry on account of their taskmasters.
Indeed, I know their sufferings, and I have come down to deliver
them from the Egyptians, and to bring them up out of that land to a
good and broad land, a land flowing with milk and honey.'

Reflection

God called Moses to set his people free. They had become slaves in Egypt. It had happened very slowly and they had hardly noticed the changes, but now they were trapped by Pharaoh, king of Egypt. God calls to Moses to be his messenger, to lead the people of Israel out of slavery to freedom in the Promised Land. God made us to be free, to break the chains that trap us. Moses prepared the way for Jesus by standing up for freedom. How can we be free?

Prayer

God, you always hear the cries of your people,
when we are unhappy or in trouble.
Come to us, help us to break free from all that binds us,
and bring us safely to our promised land,
through Jesus, who is the shoot from the stump of Jesse.
Amen.

The symbol for Moses is hung on the Jesse Tree.

Ruth and Boaz – crossing cultures

Bible Reading – *Ruth 2.1–7*

Now Naomi had a kinsman on her husband's side, a prominent rich man, of the family of Elimelech, whose name was Boaz. And Ruth the Moabite said to Naomi, 'Let me go to the field and glean among the ears of grain, behind someone in whose sight I may find favour.' She said to her, 'Go, my daughter.' So she went. She came and gleaned in the field behind the reapers. As it happened, she came to the part of the field belonging to Boaz, who was of the family of Elimelech. Just then Boaz came from Bethlehem. He said to the reapers, 'The Lord be with you.' They answered, 'The Lord bless you.' Then Boaz said to his servant who was in charge of the reapers, 'To whom does this young woman belong?' The servant who was in charge of the reapers answered, 'She is the Moabite who came back with Naomi from the country of Moab. She said, "Please, let me glean and gather among the sheaves behind the reapers." So she came, and she has been on her feet from early this morning until now, without resting even for a moment.'

Reflection

Ruth was a foreigner. She had married Naomi's son but he had died. She has chosen to stay with Naomi: 'Where you go, I will go; where you lodge, I will lodge; your people shall be my people, and your God my God' (Ruth 1.16). Boaz sees how hard she works, he sees how loyal she is, and he protects her. Later they would be married! Ruth shows us how love can break down barriers between different peoples and nations. She prepares the way for Jesus by showing that God's love is meant for everyone, not just a few. Can we be like Ruth and Boaz in the way we break down divisions?

Prayer

God, you call us to love like you,
to love with an open heart,
to break down barriers and divisions.
Help us to be bridge-builders and peacemakers,
through Jesus, who is the shoot from the stump of Jesse.
Amen.

The symbol for Ruth and Boaz is hung on the Jesse Tree.

Hymn/Song – *suggestions*

Make me a channel of your peace, Sebastian Temple

The Spirit lives to set us free, Damian Lundy

David the Shepherd – becoming King

Bible Reading – *1 Samuel 16.1, 4–7, 10–13*

The Lord said to Samuel, 'How long will you grieve over Saul? I have rejected him from being king over Israel. Fill your horn with oil and set out; I will send you to Jesse the Bethlehemite, for I have provided for myself a king among his sons.'

Samuel did what the Lord commanded, and came to Bethlehem. The elders of the city came to meet him trembling, and said, 'Do you come peaceably?' He said, 'Peaceably; I have come to sacrifice to the Lord; sanctify yourselves and come with me to the sacrifice.' And he sanctified Jesse and his sons and invited them to the sacrifice.

When they came, he looked on Eliab and thought, 'Surely the Lord's anointed is now before the Lord.' But the Lord said to Samuel, 'Do not look on his appearance or on the height of his stature, because I have rejected him; for the Lord does not see as mortals see; they look on the outward appearance, but the Lord looks on the heart.'

Jesse made seven of his sons pass before Samuel, and Samuel said to Jesse, 'The Lord has not chosen any of these.' Samuel said to Jesse, 'Are all your sons here?' And he said, 'There remains yet the youngest, but he is keeping the sheep.' And Samuel said to Jesse, 'Send and bring him; for we will not sit down until he comes here.' He sent and brought him in. Now he was ruddy, and had beautiful eyes, and was handsome. The Lord said, 'Rise and anoint him; for this is the one.' Then Samuel took the horn of oil, and anointed him in the presence of his brothers; and the spirit of the Lord came mightily upon David from that day forward.

Reflection

Samuel was a wise and faithful messenger of God but he had an important lesson to learn. He thought that a king needs to be powerful and strong but God reminded him that people look on the outside, whereas God looks on the heart. Jesse didn't even think to present his youngest son, David, who was out watching the sheep. But God chose David to be king, the least likely of all the brothers. David prepared the way for Jesus to come by showing us that God looks on our inner qualities, not what we look like on the outside. Can we learn to see through God's eyes?

Prayer

God, you called David from the very lowliest job
to be the greatest king of Israel.
Help us to see with your eyes,
not looking at the outward appearance but at the heart,
through Jesus, who is the shoot from the stump of Jesse.
Amen.

The symbol for David is hung on the Jesse Tree.

Solomon the Wise – building a Temple

Bible Reading – *1 Kings 5.2–5*

Solomon sent word to Hiram, saying, 'You know that my father David could not build a house for the name of the Lord his God because of the warfare with which his enemies surrounded him, until the Lord put them under the soles of his feet. But now the Lord my God has given me rest on every side; there is neither adversary nor misfortune. So I intend to build a house for the name of the Lord my God, as the Lord said to my father David, "Your son, whom I will set on your throne in your place, shall build the house for my name."'

Reflection

Solomon was the son of King David. He was a wise king, and the kingdom was peaceful. He decided to build a house for the Lord, a temple for God. It was made of the best materials and decorated with the finest gold. Solomon wanted to show the world how important God was to him, and to have a place where people could come to worship God. Hundreds of years later the disciples were admiring the stones and the building of the temple, and Jesus warned them that all this would be torn down. The real temple for God is the human heart! Can we live in a way that honours God, to be a living temple?

Prayer

God, you cannot be contained in temples and churches.
You are the creator of the whole universe!
Help us to worship you in spirit and in truth,
to be a living temple for your presence in us,
through Jesus, who is the shoot from the stump of Jesse.
Amen.

The symbol for Solomon is hung on the Jesse Tree.

Hymn/Song – *suggestions*

The Lord's my Shepherd, Stuart Townend

Jesus put this song into our hearts, Graham Kendrick

Isaiah the Exile – prophecy of a Saviour

Bible Reading – *Isaiah 9.2, 6–7*

The people who walked in darkness
have seen a great light;
those who lived in a land of deep darkness –
on them light has shined.
For a child has been born for us,
a son given to us;
authority rests upon his shoulders;
and he is named Wonderful Counsellor, Mighty God,
Everlasting Father, Prince of Peace.
His authority shall grow continually,
and there shall be endless peace
for the throne of David and his kingdom.
He will establish and uphold it

with justice and with righteousness
from this time onwards and for evermore.
The zeal of the Lord of hosts will do this.

Reflection

The people of Israel had been invaded and carried off into exile, their cities burned and their temple destroyed. Everything seemed to have gone wrong. What were they to do? The prophet Isaiah spoke words of hope: that they would be restored to their own land one day and would rebuild their country. He spoke of a special child who would be born, a child who would save his people. Isaiah was preparing the way for the coming of Jesus, who would be the Saviour of the world. Can we be people who hope for a better future?

Prayer

God, even in the darkest days, when everything has gone wrong,
you send your word of hope to lead us through.
Help us to be people of hope, looking for the coming of your Son,
who will be called the Prince of Peace,
through Jesus, who is the shoot from the stump of Jesse.
Amen.

The symbol for Isaiah is hung on the Jesse Tree.

John the Baptist – preparing the Way

Bible Reading – *Matthew 3.1–6*

In those days John the Baptist appeared in the wilderness of Judea, proclaiming, 'Repent, for the kingdom of heaven has come near.' This is the one of whom the prophet Isaiah spoke when he said, 'The voice of one crying out in the wilderness: "Prepare the way of the Lord, make his paths straight."' Now John wore clothing of camel's hair with a leather belt around his waist, and his food was locusts and wild honey. Then the people of Jerusalem and all Judea were going out to him, and all the region along the Jordan, and they were baptized by him in the river Jordan, confessing their sins.

Reflection

John the Baptist lived at the same time as Jesus, and he called people to the river Jordan to be baptized, to wash away their old lives and to begin again with God. Even Jesus came to be baptized by John. John was not afraid to speak up about what was right and wrong, but the powerful King Herod did not like being criticized, so he had John arrested and later killed. John came to prepare the way for Jesus. Can we be brave like him and stand up for what is right?

Prayer

God, you called John the Baptist to prepare the way.
He pointed to Jesus and away from himself.
Help us to be like John, to point others towards Jesus
and to stand up for what we know to be right,
through Jesus, who is the shoot from the stump of Jesse.
Amen.

The symbol for John the Baptist is hung on the Jesse Tree.

Mary and Gabriel – saying yes to God

Bible Reading – *Luke 1.26–32, 38*

In the sixth month the angel Gabriel was sent by God to a town in Galilee called Nazareth, to a virgin engaged to a man whose name was Joseph, of the house of David. The virgin's name was Mary. And he came to her and said, 'Greetings, favoured one! The Lord is with you.' But she was much perplexed by his words and pondered what sort of greeting this might be. The angel said to her, 'Do not be afraid, Mary, for you have found favour with God. And now, you will conceive in your womb and bear a son, and you will name him Jesus. He will be great, and will be called the Son of the Most High,

and the Lord God will give to him the throne of his ancestor David.'
Then Mary said, 'Here am I, the servant of the Lord; let it be with me
according to your word.' Then the angel departed from her.

Reflection

At last the time was right. God sent his messenger, Gabriel, to a young
woman called Mary. His strange announcement was that she would
have a baby, who would be called the Son of God, and his name would
be Jesus. Mary listened and understood that this was God's plan to
bring us back to God, and she said yes: 'Let it be with me according to
your word.' Mary prepared the way for Jesus to come into the world.
Can we say 'yes' to God in our lives?

Prayer

God, you ask us to become part of your family,
to allow Jesus to live in our lives.
Help us to hear your voice leading us,
and, with Mary, to say 'yes' to you,
through Jesus, who is the shoot from the stump of Jesse.
Amen.

The symbol for Mary is hung on the Jesse Tree.

Jesus – a new beginning

Bible Reading – *John 1.1–5*

In the beginning was the Word, and the Word was with God, and the
Word was God. He was in the beginning with God. All things came
into being through him, and without him not one thing came into
being. What has come into being in him was life, and the life was the
light of all people. The light shines in the darkness, and the darkness
did not overcome it.

Reflection

Jesus was the Word of God – from the very beginning, the light of the world that could never be put out. Jesus was God's answer to all that had gone wrong in our world, the one who came to set us free and to lead us home. From the very beginning, God has reached out to us, through countless generations who have prepared the way for Jesus to come. Can we prepare our hearts to welcome his coming, this Christmas?

Prayer

God, you love the world so much
that you sent your own son to be our Saviour,
to show us the way to come home to you.
As we complete our Jesse Tree,
help us to rejoice with all who prepared the way for Jesus to come.
Amen.

The symbol for Jesus is hung on the Jesse Tree.

We say the Lord's prayer together:

**Our Father, who art in heaven,
hallowed be thy name;
thy kingdom come;
thy will be done;
on earth as it is in heaven.
Give us this day our daily bread.
And forgive us our trespasses,
as we forgive those who trespass against us.
And lead us not into temptation;
but deliver us from evil.
For thine is the kingdom,
the power and the glory,
for ever and ever.
Amen.**

Hymn/Song – *suggestions*

O come, O come, Emmanuel, tr. John Mason Neale

Great is the darkness, Noel Richards

Blessing

God of all time,
you span the generations with your love,
calling us home to you.
Bless us now as we prepare the way of the Lord
and welcome Jesus to be our Saviour.
May the blessing of God,
Father, Son and Holy Spirit,
be with us now and always.
Amen.

What's in a Name?

Advent – Exploring holy wisdom,
the unfolding name of God

and his name shall be called
Wonderful,
Counsellor,
The mighty God,
The everlasting Father,
The Prince of Peace.

Preparation and Invitation

*This service can be held at any time in Advent. You will need readers
for each of the Bible passages. Introductory parts and prayers may be
shared among other service leaders. If you have a choir or singers, you
may like to invite them to insert some anthems or other songs instead
of carols.*

*Depending on the length of service you want to plan, you may like
to leave out some of the sections.*

Gathering Music – *suggestion*

Messiah – For unto us a child is born, George Frideric Handel

Welcome and Introduction

Advent and Christmas present us with a rich tapestry as we recall how
God reveals himself to us. The name of God has always been held to be
sacred, not to be used lightly – a means of God's self-revelation to his
people. The ten commandments warn against taking the name of the

Lord in vain. The Lord's Prayer begins 'hallowed be thy name'. Today we will explore some of the names by which God has revealed himself to human beings as we seek to enter the mystery of God's presence.

Opening Prayer

Name above all names,
Living Word of God,
Spirit of Truth,
be with us now,
open our hearts and our minds
as we come to worship you,
in the name of Jesus,
our Saviour and our King.
Amen.

Hymn/Song – *suggestions*

> Of the Father's love begotten, tr. Henry Williams Baker and John Mason Neale
>
> Joy to the world, Isaac Watts

First Lesson

The prophet Isaiah offered words of hope to a people long exiled from their home, who longed for peace and to return home. Isaiah reminded them of the names and the character of their God.

> The people who walked in darkness
> have seen a great light;
> those who lived in a land of deep darkness –
> on them light has shined.
> You have multiplied the nation,
> you have increased its joy;
> they rejoice before you
> as with joy at the harvest,
> as people exult when dividing plunder.
> For the yoke of their burden,
> and the bar across their shoulders,
> the rod of their oppressor,

you have broken as on the day of Midian.
For all the boots of the tramping warriors
and all the garments rolled in blood
shall be burned as fuel for the fire.
For a child has been born for us,
a son given to us;
authority rests upon his shoulders;
and he is named
Wonderful Counsellor, Mighty God,
Everlasting Father, Prince of Peace.
His authority shall grow continually,
and there shall be endless peace
for the throne of David and his kingdom.
He will establish and uphold it
with justice and with righteousness
from this time onwards and for evermore.
The zeal of the Lord of hosts will do this.
Isaiah 9.2–7

Prayer

God of hope,
when we are far from home,
when we have lost our way,
speak to us your holy name,
draw us back to you,
to find in you our way, our truth and our life,
through Jesus Christ our Lord.
Amen.

Hymn/Song – *suggestions*

The people that in darkness sat, John Morison

Great is the darkness, Noel Richards

Second Lesson

'Wonderful Counsellor' is a name that reminds us of the wonder and the wisdom of God. God's wisdom guides and counsels us through all our lives. In the book of Proverbs, 'Holy Wisdom' is with God in the very act of creation, delighting in the human race.

The Lord created me at the beginning of his work,
the first of his acts of long ago.
Ages ago I was set up,
at the first, before the beginning of the earth.
When there were no depths I was brought forth,
when there were no springs abounding with water.
Before the mountains had been shaped,
before the hills, I was brought forth –
when he had not yet made earth and fields,
or the world's first bits of soil.
When he established the heavens, I was there,
when he drew a circle on the face of the deep,
when he made firm the skies above,
when he established the fountains of the deep,
when he assigned to the sea its limit,
so that the waters might not transgress his command,
when he marked out the foundations of the earth,
then I was beside him, like a master worker;
and I was daily his delight,
rejoicing before him always,
rejoicing in his inhabited world
and delighting in the human race.
Proverbs 8.22–31

Prayer

God of wonder and wisdom,
inspiring us with the wonders of the universe,
guiding us with the wisdom of the ages,
be with us now as we call on you
to be our Wonderful Counsellor,
through Jesus Christ our Lord.
Amen.

Hymn/Song – *suggestions*

Immortal, invisible, God only wise, Walter Chalmers Smith

Praise the source of faith and learning, Thomas H. Troeger

Third Lesson

'Wonderful Counsellor' is also a name that we hear echoed in the coming of the Holy Spirit, when Jesus promises to send another Advocate – another Comforter, another Counsellor, another Paraclete. This is the Spirit of truth who will lead us into all truth.

Jesus said, 'If you love me, you will keep my commandments. And I will ask the Father, and he will give you another Advocate, to be with you for ever. This is the Spirit of truth, whom the world cannot receive, because it neither sees him nor knows him. You know him, because he abides with you, and he will be in you.'
John 14.15–17

Prayer

Holy Spirit of God,
breath of life and fire of love,
you awake in us every good gift,
calling and equipping us for service.
Be with us now as we call on you
to be our Wonderful Counsellor,
through Jesus Christ our Lord.
Amen.

Hymn/Song – *suggestions*

Come, Holy Spirit, come, Michael Forster

A great and mighty wonder, tr. John Mason Neale

Fourth Lesson

'Mighty God' is a name that recalls the very earliest names revealed in the Old Testament. The Hebrew people called upon Elohim, Adonai and El Shaddai; all these names point to the power and might of God, a strong God who can inspire fear and command obedience.

As Pharaoh drew near, the Israelites looked back, and there were the Egyptians advancing on them. In great fear the Israelites cried out to the Lord. They said to Moses, 'Was it because there were no graves in Egypt that you have taken us away to die in the wilderness? What have you done to us, bringing us out of Egypt? Is this not the very thing we told you in Egypt, "Let us alone and let us serve the Egyptians"? For it would have been better for us to serve the Egyptians than to die in the wilderness.' But Moses said to the people, 'Do not be afraid, stand firm, and see the deliverance that the Lord will accomplish for you today; for the Egyptians whom you see today you shall never see again. The Lord will fight for you, and you have only to keep still.'
Exodus 14.10–14

Prayer

Almighty God, who holds the universe in being,
giving energy and life to all that is
and giving us freedom to become what we may,
be with us now as we call on you
to be our Mighty God,
through Jesus Christ our Lord.
Amen.

Hymn/Song – *suggestions*

A mighty fortress is our God, Martin Luther

Name of all majesty, Timothy Dudley-Smith

Fifth Lesson

'Mighty God' is also a name that Jesus revealed in a new way, showing God's power made perfect in humble service: being born in a humble stable, kneeling and washing his disciples' feet and giving his life for us on the cross. The self-emptying of God shows true might and power through vulnerability and service.

> Let the same mind be in you that was in Christ Jesus,
> who, though he was in the form of God,
> did not regard equality with God
> as something to be exploited,
> but emptied himself,
> taking the form of a slave,
> being born in human likeness.
> And being found in human form,
> he humbled himself
> and became obedient to the point of death –
> even death on a cross.
> Therefore God also highly exalted him
> and gave him the name
> that is above every name,
> so that at the name of Jesus
> every knee should bend,
> in heaven and on earth and under the earth,
> and every tongue should confess
> that Jesus Christ is Lord,
> to the glory of God the Father.
> *Philippians 2.5–11*

Prayer

Self-emptying God,
you pour yourself into creation,
holding nothing back,
giving everything.
Be with us now as we call on you
to be our Mighty God,
through Jesus Christ our Lord.
Amen.

Hymn/Song – *suggestions*

Morning glory, starlit sky, William Hubert Vanstone

Meekness and majesty, Graham Kendrick

Sixth Lesson

'Everlasting Father' is a name that reminds us that God is eternal, outside time, infinite. We are so linear, so finite in our thinking, that we find it hard to imagine anything to be everlasting. We are caught up in a world of time. There is a time for everything under heaven.

> For everything there is a season, and a time for every matter
>   under heaven:
> a time to be born, and a time to die;
> a time to plant, and a time to pluck up what is planted;
> a time to kill, and a time to heal;
> a time to break down, and a time to build up;
> a time to weep, and a time to laugh;
> a time to mourn, and a time to dance;
> a time to throw away stones, and a time to gather stones together;
> a time to embrace, and a time to refrain from embracing;
> a time to seek, and a time to lose;
> a time to keep, and a time to throw away;
> a time to tear, and a time to sew;
> a time to keep silence, and a time to speak;
> a time to love, and a time to hate;
> a time for war, and a time for peace.
> *Ecclesiastes 3.1–8*

Prayer

God of time and eternity,
you give us the gift of time –
years, months, days, hours.
Give us wisdom to perceive the fitting time,
your moment when it comes.
Be with us now as we call on you
to be our Eternal Father,
through Jesus Christ our Lord.
Amen.

Hymn/Song – *suggestions*

Now is eternal life, George Wallace Briggs

O, the love of my Lord is the essence, Estelle White

Seventh Lesson

'Eternal Father' is a name that reminds us of the incredible intimacy of Jesus' relationship with God. He taught us to say 'Our Father', and in his own prayers called God by the intimate form of 'Abba'. We are invited into this intimate relationship, to know God as Abba our heavenly Father, who has adopted us as his children.

My point is this: heirs, as long as they are minors, are no better than slaves, though they are the owners of all the property; but they remain under guardians and trustees until the date set by the father. So with us; while we were minors, we were enslaved to the elemental spirits of the world. But when the fullness of time had come, God sent his Son, born of a woman, born under the law, in order to redeem those who were under the law, so that we might receive adoption as children. And because you are children, God has sent the Spirit of his Son into our hearts, crying, 'Abba! Father!' So you are no longer a slave but a child, and if a child then also an heir, through God.
Galatians 4.1–7

Prayer

Abba, Father, you run towards us
with outstretched arms to welcome us home,
you lift us when we fall, you bind up our wounds,
you embrace us in your love.
Be with us now as we call on you
to be our Eternal Father,
through Jesus Christ our Lord.
Amen.

Hymn/Song – *suggestions*

Father most holy, merciful and loving, tr. Alfred Edward Alston

Lead us, heavenly Father, lead us, James Edmeston

Eighth Lesson

'Prince of Peace' is a name that speaks to us of Jesus promising his disciples that his kingdom will be one of peace, which this world cannot give. He taught us how to forgive and be reconciled, to make peace. In the Beatitudes he called peacemakers the children of God.

> When Jesus saw the crowds, he went up the mountain; and after he sat down, his disciples came to him. Then he began to speak, and taught them, saying:
> 'Blessed are the poor in spirit, for theirs is the kingdom of heaven.
> 'Blessed are those who mourn, for they will be comforted.
> 'Blessed are the meek, for they will inherit the earth.
> 'Blessed are those who hunger and thirst for righteousness, for they will be filled.
> 'Blessed are the merciful, for they will receive mercy.
> 'Blessed are the pure in heart, for they will see God.
> 'Blessed are the peacemakers, for they will be called children of God.
> 'Blessed are those who are persecuted for righteousness' sake, for theirs is the kingdom of heaven.
> 'Blessed are you when people revile you and persecute you and utter all kinds of evil against you falsely on my account. Rejoice and be glad, for your reward is great in heaven, for in the same way they persecuted the prophets who were before you.'
> *Matthew 5.1–12*

Prayer

God who calms the storms,
bring your peace to our troubled world.
God who speaks in the still, small voice of calm,
breathe through the heats of our desires
and help us to be peacemakers.
Be with us now as we call on you
to be our Prince of Peace,
through Jesus Christ our Lord.
Amen.

Hymn/Song – *suggestions*

Dear Lord and Father of mankind, John Greenleaf Whittier

Be still for the presence of the Lord, David J. Evans

Ninth Lesson

The most sacred name of God in the Hebrew Bible is the name given by God to Moses, too holy to be spoken or written: YHWH, which we have pronounced Yahweh or Jehovah. It is translated 'I am who I am', a mystery, an enigma, always beyond our comprehension yet revealed to us that we might know God.

But Moses said to God, 'If I come to the Israelites and say to them, "The God of your ancestors has sent me to you", and they ask me, "What is his name?" what shall I say to them?' God said to Moses, 'I am who I am.' He said further, 'Thus you shall say to the Israelites, "I am has sent me to you."' God also said to Moses, 'Thus you shall say to the Israelites, "The Lord, the God of your ancestors, the God of Abraham, the God of Isaac, and the God of Jacob, has sent me to you": This is my name for ever, and this my title for all generations.'
Exodus 3.13–15

Prayer

God of mystery,
always beyond our comprehension,
immortal, invisible, hid from our eyes
yet coming close to reveal yourself to us,
be with us now as we call on you
to be who you will be, the great 'I AM',
through Jesus Christ our Lord.
Amen.

Hymn/Song – *suggestions*

The God of Abraham praise, Thomas Olivers

How shall I sing that majesty, John Mason

Tenth Lesson

We come to the very heart of the mystery of God's self-revelation, to the birth of Jesus, foretold by the prophets, with a new name, Emmanuel, which means 'God is with us'. God identifies himself completely with us, becoming one of us, in the incarnation of the Word.

Now the birth of Jesus the Messiah took place in this way. When his mother Mary had been engaged to Joseph, but before they lived together, she was found to be with child from the Holy Spirit. Her husband Joseph, being a righteous man and unwilling to expose her to public disgrace, planned to dismiss her quietly. But just when he had resolved to do this, an angel of the Lord appeared to him in a dream and said, 'Joseph, son of David, do not be afraid to take Mary as your wife, for the child conceived in her is from the Holy Spirit. She will bear a son, and you are to name him Jesus, for he will save his people from their sins.' All this took place to fulfil what had been spoken by the Lord through the prophet: 'Look, the virgin shall conceive and bear a son, and they shall name him Emmanuel', which means, 'God is with us.' When Joseph awoke from sleep, he did as the angel of the Lord commanded him; he took her as his wife, but had no marital relations with her until she had borne a son; and he named him Jesus.
Matthew 1.18–25

Prayer

God with us,
God one of us,
God in us,
as we contemplate your holy name,
help us to grow into your likeness.
Be with us now as we call on you
and greet you as Emmanuel,
Jesus Christ our Lord.
Amen.

Responses

No one has ever seen God;
if we love one another,
God lives in us,

and his love is perfected in us.
God is love,
and those who abide in love abide in God,
and God abides in them.

1 John 4.12, 16

Our Father, who art in heaven,
hallowed be thy name;
thy kingdom come;
thy will be done;
on earth as it is in heaven.
Give us this day our daily bread.
And forgive us our trespasses,
as we forgive those
who trespass against us.
And lead us not into temptation;
but deliver us from evil.
For thine is the kingdom,
the power and the glory,
for ever and ever.
Amen.

Blessing

Name above every name,
dwell in our hearts.
Jesus the human face of divine love,
bring peace in our world.
Spirit who awakens us to life's wonder and mystery,
bring us your blessing,
now and always.
May the blessing of God, Father, Son and Spirit
be with us now and for ever.
Amen.

Hymn/Song – *suggestions*

O come, O come, Emmanuel, tr. John Mason Neale

Lo! He comes with clouds descending, Charles Wesley

Resources

Warhorse – Ploughing theme, John Williams
www.amazon.com/War-Horse-John-Williams/dp/B005LK8NSK

'Daily Bread', Malcolm Guite, from *Parable and Paradox*, Canterbury Press, 2016

Goodness of God, Jenn Johnson
https://holymusik.com/goodness-of-god-jenn-bethel-mp3/

Nunc dimittis, Geoffrey Burgon
www.amazon.co.uk/Nunc-Dimittis-Tinker-Tailor-Soldier/dp/B0029RL3IA

All-Night Vigil – Nunc Dimittis, Sergei Rachmaninoff, sung by Katie Melua
www.amazon.de/Winter-Katie-Melua/dp/B01KME6IBS

Let all the world in every corner sing, William Walton
www.hyperion-records.co.uk/dw.asp?dc=W4899_GBAJY0233021

Who would true valour see, Maddy Prior and the Carnival Band
www.amazon.co.uk/Would-True-Valour-John-Bunyan/dp/B0170JGYYY

Hymn to the Mother of God, John Tavener
www.hyperion-records.co.uk/dw.asp?dc=W3863_66464

'Mothering Sunday', Malcolm Guite, from *Sounding the Seasons*, Canterbury Press, 2012

Blackbird, The Beatles
https://archive.org/details/111Blackbird

Goldberg Variations, BWV 988 – Aria, Johann Sebastian Bach
www.openculture.com/2012/05/the_open_goldberg_variations.html

Chasing sheep is best left to shepherds, Michael Nyman
www.amazon.co.uk/Chasing-Sheep-Best-Left-Shepherds/dp/
B01AAVIECY

Prelude and fugue in F major, BWV556, Johann Sebastian Bach
www.amazon.co.uk/dp/B001N04LLK/ref=dm_ws_tlw_trk10

All things bright and beautiful, John Rutter
www.hyperion-records.co.uk/dw.asp?dc=W18690_GBAKR0012614

A prayer of St Richard of Chichester, Michael Leighton Jones
www.amazon.co.uk/dp/B07C61LZTJ/ref=dm_ws_tlw_trk5

In an English country garden, eighteenth-century folk tune, arr. Percy
Grainger
www.amazon.co.uk/English-Country-Garden/dp/B0089CE11U

D'un vieux jardin, Lili Boulanger
www.amazon.co.uk/s?k=D%E2%80%99un+vieux+jardin%3A+Lili+
Boulanger&i=digital-music&ref=nb_sb_noss

The River Cam, Eric Whitacre
www.amazon.com/Whitacre-River-feat-Julian-Webber/dp/
B007MXMVW8

We're off to see the wizard, E. Y. Harburg and Harold Arlen
https://archive.org/details/WereOffToSeeTheWizard

'How Dorothy saved the scarecrow', *The Wonderful Wizard of Oz*,
L. Frank Baum
www.gutenberg.org/files/55/55-h/55-h.htm#chap03

Goldberg Variations, BWV 988 – Aria, Johann Sebastian Bach
www.classicalmpr.org/story/2019/05/10/daily-download-johann-
sebastian-bach--goldberg-variations-aria

John Barleycorn, Martin Carthy
www.amazon.com/John-Barleycorn-Live/dp/B01MS2DVMV

Maddy Prior and the Carnival Band, *Sing Lustily and with Good Courage*
www.amazon.co.uk/Lustily-Courage-Maddy-Prior-Carnival/dp/B0170JGX40

Panis angelicus, César Franck
www.hyperion-records.co.uk/dw.asp?dc=W17482_GBLLH0811511

Thou visitest the earth, Maurice Greene
www.amazon.com/Greene-Thou-Visitest-the-Earth/dp/B004ULZAX2

The Carnival of the Animals – The aquarium, Camille Saint-Saëns
www.yourclassical.org/story/2018/02/12/daily-download-camille-saintsaens--carnival-of-the-animals-aquarium

When David heard, Eric Whitacre
www.hyperion-records.co.uk/dw.asp?dc=W4444_GBAJY0654306

O magnum mysterium, Morten Lauridsen
www.hyperion-records.co.uk/tw.asp?w=W1682

Music for the Royal Fireworks, George Frideric Handel
www.deccaclassics.com/gb/cat/4145962

The Planets – Venus, the bringer of peace, Gustav Holst
www.yourclassical.org/story/2019/02/22/daily-download-gustav-holst--the-planets-venus-the-bringer-of-peace

Look at the world, John Rutter
www.hyperion-records.co.uk/dw.asp?dc=W18709_GBAKR0312906

Messiah – For unto us a child is born, George Frideric Handel
www.hyperion-records.co.uk/dw.asp?dc=W5218_67800